WHY SPROUTS?

- Because they can be grown cheaply and easily in days from a handful of seeds
- Because they concentrate—even multiply—the vitamin and protein content of your diet
- Because they are the ultimate in freshness, producing vitamins up to the instant of eating
- Because they provide the greatest variety in delicious taste—from rich, nutritious soy and alfalfa to the spicy seasoning provided by cress or black radish
- Because, when all is said and done, they are the most direct use of food—allowing you to avoid the energy-wasting "food chain" of meats and poultry

Learn all about sprouts—and what they can do for your health, your menus and your budget—in

ADD A FEW SPROUTS

ADD
A FEW
SPROUTS

To Eat Better
For Less Money

Martha H. Oliver

Keats Publishing, Inc. New Canaan, Connecticut

ADD A FEW SPROUTS

Pivot Original Health Edition published 1975

Printed in the United States of America

Library of Congress Catalog Card Number: 75-10539

PIVOT ORIGINAL HEALTH BOOKS are published by
Keats Publishing, Inc.
36 Grove Street, New Canaan, Connecticut 06840, U.S.A.

CONTENTS

INTRODUCTION

This book is not specifically for vegetarians, although they will find it a valuable guide to the solutions of some problems encountered in following a vegetarian diet. Nor is it a book only for persons who follow a health-food regime, although, again, their special requirements are readily met in the use of germinated seeds as a source of food. It is not written for lovers of Chinese foods, though these will find it an economical way to procure a necessary staple, nor for those who cannot exist without the exotic and the foreign to grace their tables every night. This book is for persons who are interested in a delicious, highly nutritious and novel vegetable that has been eaten for centuries by Eastern peoples, and which could be added to Western diets with great benefit.

Anyone who has enough shelf space to hold one jam jar (no garden space, not one teaspoon of soil is required) can grow a lovely crop of germinated seeds in three to five days, depending on the variety of seed and the temperature of the room. The seeds need only air and moisture; no chemicals, no fertilizers, no cultivation, no sunlight, no spraying, no weeding; and, after they are grown, no washing, no peeling, no chopping, no seeding, no preparation of any kind is necessary.

In addition to being easy to grow, bean sprouts are highly nutritious. They contain as much vitamin C as tomatoes, as much vitamin B as whole-wheat flour, as much protein as meat. All this can be had for two cents a serving.

Bean sprouts came into their own in our country in the 1940s, in the days of meat shortages and meat rationing. They were widely publicized at the time as a meat alternative. Dr. Clive McCay, a leading proponent of the value of sprouted soybeans, demonstrates the tone of many of the publications of the day in this oft-repeated remark: "Our daily paper would surprise us if it carried an ad: 'Wanted: a vegetable that will grow in any climate, rivals meat in nutritive value, matures in three to five days, may be planted any day of the year, requires neither soil or sunshine, rivals tomatoes in vitamin C, has no waste, can be cooked with as little fuel and as quickly as a pork chop.' The Chinese discovered this vegetable centuries ago in sprouted soybeans." (34).

This centuries-old vegetable is versatile. It can be cooked in a variety of ways with a variety of seasonings. It lends itself to combinations of old, familiar recipes, as well as to spur-of-the moment experiments. This book will give you an idea of the sort of thing that can be done with sprouts, a little of their history, a glimpse of the complex chemical changes that occur during germination and all the information you need to grow sprouts yourself.

Chapter 5 is a collection of recipes for sprouts— recipes for soups and beverages, salads, entrees, vegetable dishes, breads and stuffings, and desserts. Additional recipes may be found in many recent cookbooks. The best of these, in my opinion, are Beatrice Trum Hunter's *The Natural Foods Cookbook* and Dorothea Jones's *The Soybean Cookbook*. Each includes a section of how to sprout and a number of excellent recipes. Of recent publication are two cookbooks devoted exclusively to sprouts, both containing some fine recipes: Gay Courter's *The Beansprout Book* and Karen Cross Whyte's *The Complete Sprouting Cookbook*. These two offer excellent directions on sprouting as well as some of the most original ways to use sprouts that I've seen yet. Some books of more general interest, such as Ruth Bircher-Benner's *Eating Your Way to Health* and Mildred Lager's *The Useful Soybean*, include good recipes using sprouts.

It is to be hoped that the revival of interest in sprouting will offer more people a way to add variety to their diet, to eat better for less, and to contribute a fascinating historical concept to their knowledge of nutrition.

ADD A FEW SPROUTS

CHAPTER ONE

SPROUTS FOR ENERGY-SAVING AND NUTRITION

When you go to the market to buy food, what is the most important consideration in your mind? Food value? Taste appeal? Protein and vitamin content? Price? Perhaps the relative importance of these considerations is shifting around as another variable enters the scene—energy.

What about the energy required to produce the food?

Think of the energy consumption represented in, say, a frozen vegetable. The farmer uses oil and gas in his tractor to plow, harrow and plant. Coal derivatives are used in the seed treatment, chemical fertilizers and herbicides as the crop grows. The vegetable is harvested by machine, transported by truck and processed in a mechanized way. It is wrapped in paper or plastic, which consumed energy in its manufacture. Then it is transported to a central warehouse, held at the freezing point, and taken to the store by truck, where it is held at the proper temperature—all of which consumes energy. You drive to the store, buy it, bring it home and store it in your freezer. How many gallons of gas and oil, kilowatt hours of electricity and tons of coal have been spent in getting that vegetable on your table?

All that use of energy adds to the cost, and it is

all passed along to you! How much of the price represents the cost of the vegetable itself, and how much the cost of the energy consumed in its processing?

Like the processed vegetable, animal protein is expensive; considering the amount of food energy required to produce it, it might even be called wasteful. One quart of milk contains one-seventh the food energy of the fodder required to produce it. The chicken feed required to produce one dozen eggs contains nineteen times more calories than the eggs. What happens to the lost energy? It keeps the cow and the chickens warm and moving around. On the average 10% of the energy in plants fed to animals is harvested as meat.

From another angle, the cost of animal proteins can be reckoned in pure protein output per acre of land. One acre would produce 600 pounds of protein if grass were grown on it; from legumes (beans and peas), 370 pounds; from wheat, 269 pounds; from milk, 90 pounds; and from beef, 54 pounds. The figure for grass is still theoretical since the means to make the protein in grass commercially available to man is not yet worked out.

The amount of energy required to produce food explains why optimistic predictions of a mammoth food harvest from the sea are unrealistic. The length of food chains there intensifies the energy loss to an incredible degree. Tuna, for example, are very large fish which feed on smaller fish, which in turn devour quantities of plankton, which subsist on algae. When we eat tuna, considering the general energy loss, we are reaping in food value less than one five-hundred-thousandth of the original light energy that fell on the algae (133).

How can we escape from this expensive, energy-consuming cycle in the production of the food we eat? Most of us live where land for a garden is unavailable, and even those who can grow a few vegetables are unable to raise a cow or chickens to supplement their protein intake.

The answer may be to emulate the peoples of the East. To utilize the maximum energy from food, a grim necessity in these underdeveloped countries, they find it more efficient to feed grain straight to man than to keep animals warm and active (138). As a result, in India, China and Southeast Asian countries, animal food supplies less than 5 percent of all food calories (133).

Their consumption of animal protein has never matched that of the West. Rather than animal protein, their staple is germinated seed-sprouts—with its remarkable concentration of vitamins and protein. Actually, the great majority of the world's population depends on seeds, sprouted or unsprouted—especially rice and soybean—for their sources of protein.

Seeds contain good-quality proteins. Seeds are sometimes simply soaked and cooked, but they are more nutritious when germinated. When they are sprouted, they shuffle their amino acid make-up so that they are more efficient for the needs of a growing plant than a dormant seed would be; and this shuffling is highly beneficial from the point of view of human protein needs, too. Sprouted seeds are also more digestible than plain seeds, so one absorbs more protein from them.

Seed sprouts can well be the answer for us in coping with the high food prices and energy shortages of the 1970s. They can provide our chief nutritional needs—proteins and vitamin C—at a lower cost than we now pay. They can be produced with a small fraction of the energy required for the provision of the vegetables and animal meats that make up our diets at the present time.

The soybean, one of the chief seeds used for sprouting, has been cultivated as a principal crop for probably 5,000 years in the Orient, where it is the staple food as meat is ours. In this century, during World War I, it became important in our country, and in Europe, as a substitute for other protein foods. Today, in the 1970s, it is important to us again, as a food that can provide us nutritious meals for less money and less energy.

CHAPTER TWO

A SHORT HISTORY OF SPROUTING:

THE USE OF SPROUTED SEEDS AS MEDICINE AND FOOD

Sprouts, like the Kola nuts in Coca-Cola, were used first as a medicine. In both East Asia and Europe, sprouts were employed to cure specific illnesses, and in China the illnesses were carefully documented in the classic writing of each period. The first mention of sprouts by the Chinese is lost in the legendary past. The semi-mythical emperor Shen Nung, who is supposed to have reigned in the twenty-eighth century B.C., is, according to Chinese tradition, the Father of Husbandry and Medicine. At the foot of a mountain in the southern Shansi is the Fountain of Cereals, where Shen Nung first taught his people to till the ground and raise grain. Hence, he is known as the Divine Husbandman. He also tested the medicinal qualities of herbs and discovered medicines to cure disease; Nature had bestowed upon him the ability to recognize instantly and instinctively by the taste what was each plant's power in curing sickness. He gathered all this information into the well-known Chinese materia medica, *Shen Nung Pen Ts'ao King*, or *Classical Work on Herbal Medicines of the Emperor Shen Nung*. Unfortunately, no known copies of this book exist, but it is quoted

17

extensively in the later herbal classics, and it is usually cited as the original authoritative source of information about herbal medicine. Shen Nung is said to have died in 2697 B.C. Of course, this information is only part of tradition and must not be taken as strictly accurate. Prior to 840 B.C., an accurate chronological dating system simply does not exist. Its interest lies in the classification and use of the drugs it prescribes rather than in the strict historical accuracy of its existence.

The *Shen Nung Pen Ts'ao King* describes 365 drugs by dividing them into three classes and describing the general properties of each class. The first class is the *Kun* or sovereigns; these support human life and therefore resemble heaven. They are not poisonous; whatever quantity you take, or however long you use them, they are harmless. If you wish to lighten the body, improve the breath, and to live to an old age without growing old, make use of the drugs of the first class. Oranges, marijuana (a non-narcotic variety), mushrooms, shepherd's-purse, elm bark and licorice are all sovereigns. The second class are *Ch'en* or ministers. They support human nature and therefore resemble man; they contain no dangerous active principles but are not desirable in unlimited amounts, so discretion is advised. They are for lessening the violence of diseases and re-establishing decayed strength. They include ginger, tiger lilies, gentians, ferns and soybean sprouts. The third class consists of *Tso*, or assistants, and *Shi*, or agents. They cure diseases, and therefore resemble earth. They are very poisonous, and must not be used continuously. They drive out cold or heat from the body, correct the breath and open obstructions. They include peach kernels (which contain a cyanide-producing substance), rhododendrons and veratrum (20).

Medical classification rather than botanical taxonomy dominated the organization of works of natural history in China for centuries. The huge supplement and commentary to the *Shen Nung Pen Ts'ao King*, which was compiled about A.D. 500 by T'ao Hung King, was the first which laid down the broad lines of classification in a natural history sense, including the 365 drugs in the *Shen Nung Pen Ts'ao King* and 365 new medicines recommended by famous physicians of the Han and Wei dynasties. The T'ao Hung King supplement also gave a complete description of the plant, its location by district or province, and the general habitat (mountain, river valley, field or marsh) as well as the part of the plant used and the time of day to gather it (an important point, since the vitamin content of plants after a sunny day is much higher than after a cloudy one or in the morning). T'ao recommends adding bean sprouts to the diet for a number of maladies, such as edema with loss of sensation, cramps of the muscles, pains at the kneecaps, visceral deficiencies, digestive disorders, weakness of the lungs, roughness and spots on the skin and abnormalities of the hair (Needham, *in litt*) (99).

Each dynasty produced its own work on medicine and natural history in which the number of classifications of plants gradually increased as more sophisticated groupings were devised. By the late sixteenth century, with the presentation of Li Shih Chen's *Pen Ts'ao Kang Mu*, the greatest of all the Chinese pharmaceutical natural histories, contemporary families of plants are clearly recognizable, grouped by physiological similarities (99). This is an exhaustive work in the true Chinese sense, for it took twenty-six years of labor to complete and eighteen years of revision and rewriting. It contains two books of woodcuts, mostly borrowed from other earlier works; Li then reviews all the sources quoted and extracted, forty-two capital works on materia medica and 950 publications of medical, historical and geographical botany. A chapter on the nature and properties of medicine follows, then an enumeration of the various diseases and the medicines suitable to cure them. Li finishes with forty-seven chapters on drugs and natural objects and their use as medicines. In the same manner as the *Oxford English Dictionary*, the description of a plant consists of successive quotations from authors of various times (111).

Li gives the traditional way to prepare the sprout of the black soybean, which he regards as having the greatest medicinal value. "On a water day soak black beans in clear water, and, after the sprouts have grown, take off the hulls and dry the sprouts in the shade" (124). He lists the medicinal properties as laxative, resolvent (reducing inflammation), and constructive. He comments that sprouts have a special influence on the growth of the hair and are curative in ascites (dropsy of the abdomen) and rheumatism. Mung bean sprouts are said to be countervinous (counteracting the effects of alcohol) and antifebrile (fever reducing). Sprouted barley, or malt, is made by moistening the grain, allowing it to germinate, rubbing off the sprout (root) and grinding it into flour. It is said to be peptic, a stomachic, lenitive (easing pain), demulcent and expectorant. Its reconstructive properties were well recognized; it was much prescribed in puerperal and infantile illnesses, and especially recommended in phthisis and the childhood disease *Kän* (124).

An herbal designed for times of famine presented in the early fifteenth century, the *Chiu-Huang Pen Ts'ao*, lists the sprout of the red mung bean and the yellow soybean as suitable food, and mentions that they are cultivated in quantity in the Straits and by Chinese in Malaya (112). These two beans would not have been considered as choice as the green mung bean and the black, blue or white soybean as a source of food, but they were certainly used.

With this historical background, it is not surprising that the first use of sprouted seeds in Western Europe was a medicinal one. Herbals from the Middle Ages do not mention sprouts at all, and the only way in which malt was used seems to be as a raw material for beer. An enterprising physician, Dr. David MacBride, was the first European to publish an opinion on the medical properties of sprouted seeds, and his thinking had been influenced by a frantic search for a cure for what was quickly becoming the scourge of eighteenth-century ocean voyages: the dreaded sea-scurvy. For centuries, oceanic exploration had followed the pattern set by the ancient Greeks; short voyages, usually within a few days' journey to a known shore where fresh water and food could be had, were the rule. The century that opened the New World and the South Seas to exploration saw a major change in the whole concept of the ocean voyage. Now ships set out in groups, prepared to spend years on their journey, sometimes for months on the open seas without any sight of land. Preparations had to be elaborate, but the diet of the sailor, in those days before refrigeration, consisted with monotonous regularity of ship biscuit, dried meat, and grog. The biscuit was usually a mass of weevils, and the meat sometimes riddled with maggots, but even the vitamins supplied by these undesirable additions were insufficient to prevent severe nutritional deficiencies. Lack of vitamin C, found only in fresh fruits and vegetables, causes a disease called scurvy. Early symptoms of scurvy were swollen, bleeding gums, a tendency to bruise easily and soreness in the joints. Usually in the advanced stages the teeth fell out, internal hemorrhages discolored the skin as blood vessels broke, the joints became so agonizingly painful that the victim screamed when touched or moved, and death followed inevitably. A contemporary epic poem describing Vasco da Gama's voyage of exploration around the Cape of Good Hope in 1497 vividly portrays the horrors of scurvy:

> A dread disease its rankling horrors shed,
> And death's dire ravage through mine army
>   spread;
> Never mine eyes such drearly sight beheld:
> Ghastly the mouths and gums enormous
>   swelled,
> And instant, putrid like a dead man's wound
> Poisoned with fetid streams the air around.
> No sage physician's ever watchful zeal,
> No skilled surgeon's gentle hand to heal
> Were found; each dreary mournful hour we
>   gave
> Some brave companion to a foreign grave.
>   From *Lusiad* by Camoëns (114)

Over half of da Gama's crew died of scurvy during the voyage, and similar losses were recorded on the famous voyages of Magellan in 1519, Jacques Cartier in 1536 and the catastrophic expedition of Lord Anson in 1741, in which of 961 sailors leaving England, 626 died of scurvy and associated maladies by the time they reached their destination, Juan Fernández, an island group off the west coast of South America (3). In 1781, one man in seven died of scurvy in the British Navy; a famous naval physician, Sir Richard Hopkins, recorded that he could give an account of ten thousand mariners who died of scurvy during the twenty years of his practice (38).

In this context, the achievement of Captain James Cook seems nearly miraculous; remember that these losses were considered unavoidable at that time. On the long voyage of the *Endeavour*, which embarked at Plymouth August 26, 1768 and anchored in the Downs July 13, 1771, a period of almost three years, not a single death from scurvy occurred. On his voyage to the Indies from July of 1772 to 1775 with the *Resolution* and *Adventure*, he had a few slight cases of the disease, but not one life was lost (3). Cook himself realized that his geographical discoveries, however remarkable, were less significant than this demonstration that a long ocean voyage need not be fatal to a large proportion of the crew. The final entry in his journal, dated July, 1775, reads, "But whatever may be the public judgement about other matters, it is with real satisfaction, and without claiming any merit but that of attention to duty, that I can conclude this Account with an observation, which facts enable me to make, that our having discovered the possibility of preserving health amongst a numerous ship's company, for such a length of time, in such varieties of climate, and amid such continued hardships and fatigues, will make this voyage remarkable in the opinion of every benevolent person, when the disputes about a Southern Continent shall have ceased to engage the attention, and to divide the judgement of philosophers" (38). The Royal Society of London, at their anniversary meeting on November 30, 1776, presented Captain Cook with their highest award, the Copley Medal, not for his discoveries on the South Seas, but for "the most useful and most successful experimental inquiry." The citation continues, "Now what inquiry can be so useful as that which hath for its object the saving the lives of men? And when shall we find one more successful than that before us? Here are no vain boastings of the empiric, nor ingenious and delusive theories of the dogmatist, but a concise, an artless, and an incontested relation of the means, by which, *under the Divine Favour, Captain Cook, with a company of an hundred and eighteen men, performed a voyage of three years and eighteen days, throughout all the climates, from fifty-two degrees north, to seventy-one degrees south, with the loss of only one man by a distemper.* [Citation's italics] What must enhance to us the value of these salutary observations, is to see the practice hath been no less simple than efficacious" (38).

In 1767, Dr. MacBride's treatise on the seascurvy had been published, with his recommendations for treatment and prevention, and Cook had been so impressed by its reasoning that he carried them out exactly. The fact that Dr. MacBride's reasoning was wrong was not surprising. Vitamin C was not to be isolated and synthesized until 1932: the good doctor had never heard of vitamins at all. He had observed, rather shrewdly, that fresh vegetables and fruits and juices prepared from them had an almost miraculous effect on scurvy. He had concluded that fresh vegetables owed their anti-scorbutic powers to their "fixed air, or ability to ferment in the bowels," by the "antiseptic powers of which the strong tendency to putrefaction in this disease might be corrected" (88). In other words, the gas-forming potential of vegetables prevented the rotting of the tissues that always accompanied scurvy.

In one sense, vitamin C does do just that that; its ability to increase the strength and elasticity of blood vessels can lessen bruising, and prevent internal and external hemorrhage. The mechanism by which this is accomplished is not really understood yet; it is safe to say, however, that it is not the antiseptic property of the fixed air in the bowels, but a complicated enzymatic reaction that takes place long before the food reaches the bowels. Dr. MacBride's thinking on the differences between raw grain and malted grain comes much closer to the truth; he understood the degradation of starch and its conversion to sugar, although he didn't call it that: "by the germination, drying and slight torrefaction, its natural viscidity is destroyed, it acquires an agreeable, saccharine taste, and the farinaceous part is so attenuated as to be rendered soluble in water. Fresh *Wort*, or *infusion of malt*, is a liquor similar to the recent juices of the sweet [i.e., not starch] vegetables, fermenting readily like them, and being precisely of the same mild, saponaceous and aperient nature" (88). He goes on to specify the best way to prepare this medicinal sweetwort, the raw material commonly used in the preparation of beer and therefore very familiar to most people. The surgeon of the *Resolution*, Mr.

Patton, recorded Dr. MacBride's observations in his journal: "I have found the *wort* of the utmost service in all scorbutic cases during the voyage. As many took it by way of prevention, few cases occured where it had a fair trial; but these, however, I flatter myself, will be sufficient to convince every impartial person, that it is the best remedy hitherto found out for the cure of the sea-scurvy; and I am well convinced, from what I have seen the *wort* perform, and from its mode of operation, that if aided by *portable-soup, sour-krout, sugar, sago,* and *courants,* the scurvy, that maritime pestilence, will seldom or never make its alarming appearance among a ship's crew, on the longest voyages . . ." (38). Sir Joseph Banks, the official botanist on the *Endeavour,* wrote in his journal, ". . . and of this [wort] I drank a pint or more every evening . . ." (66). He also used it mixed with wheat for breakfast to make frumenty, and records, "I receiv'd great benefit from the use of this mess, it totally banish'd in me that troublesome costiveness which I believe most people are subject to when at sea" (15). Constipation was an early symptom of scurvy.

The preparation of wort is simple, since most of it is done on shore. A quantity of barley or mixed grains is moistened until it sprouts; when the new leaves have just begun to appear, a stage well known to the experienced maltster, the barley is dried and heated gently to 90-140°F., just enough to inactivate the enzymes that have converted the starch of the grain to sugars. The malt is then ground and stored.

Each day on board ship the infusion was freshly prepared; MacBride writes, "the method in which it is proposed to prepare the *wort,* is, to take *one* measure of the *ground malt*, and pour it on *three* measures of boiling water; stir them well, and let the mixture stand, close covered up, for three or four hours; after which, strain off the liquor. It must be brewed, in hot weather especially, fresh every day, for if it be allowed to grow vapid, or sourish, it will not only be unpleasant, but useless, as it would then not run easily into fermentation; but when perfectly fresh, there cannot well be a more palatable kind of drink; and I dare say, that in general, it will sit light and easy on the stomach" (88).

Captain Cook's malt held out well the first two years, but by the third had lost much of its taste, and, at this point, he doubted whether it retained its potency. Mr. Patton continued to find it useful by the expedient of mixing the proportions a little stronger, although he records that it was "sensibly decayed" (38).

This method of preparation would have preserved a great deal of the vitamin C in the malt and, perhaps more important, the B-complex factor, which increases tremendously during sprouting. There is good evidence that preserved malt may contain a great deal of vitamin C (56), and beer was regarded as a potent antiscorbutic well into the twentieth century (119). The B vitamins have been found to increase the efficiency and curative powers of vitamin C (39); less vitamin C is required to reduce stress conditions in the body when B vitamins are present. Since these vitamins dissolve readily in water, they would be present in great quantity in the wort. It is fortunate that Dr. MacBride specified that the infusion was to be steeped, rather than boiled, for three hours; the boiling temperature would have destroyed most of the vitamin C and several of the B vitamins.

Captain Cook also carried a quantity of concentrated lemon juice as an alternative antiscorbutic. It had been reduced in volume by two-thirds through boiling for easy storage; this treatment would have been so destructive to the heat-labile vitamin C that Cook himself declared it less potent in "antiscorbutic stuff" than the sweetwort, and, of course, it contained no B vitamins at all.

MacBride's early attempts to test his theories had met with great difficulty, and were even considered failures. A contemporary report describes the problems and final success; the writer, trying to be impartial, is obviously very impressed. "In 1762, the Lords of the Admiralty gave orders to have the wort tried in the Naval hospitals at Portsmouth and Plymouth; but the murmurs of the patients, on account of restrictions that were necessary for determining its efficacy, put a stop to the farther exhibition of it; and indeed, Dr. Huxham, in 1764, informed the ingenious and benevolent proposer of this remedy, that it had been tried with very bad effects. But Dr. MacBride assures us, on the testimony of a gentleman who made use of the wort, that it may be taken for a length of time, to the quantity of a quart in the day, without producing any ill effects whatever; and he refers to Van Swieten's Commentary, vol. IV, p. 673, where we learn, that the baron's lady, when a nurse, used regularly to drink a pint of it every night going to bed, in order to increase her milk." (113) This remark represents sound reasoning; the B-complex vitamins are known to increase lactation. Two of the B-complex, when first isolated, were called lactation vitamins until they were properly classified (41).

"After the failure of success in the Naval hospitals, orders were issued to have the wort administered on shipboard, where no temptations of fresh vegetables would offer to make the men uneasy. But a considerable time elapsed before any reports were made either of its good or bad effects. Dr. MacBride, however, persisted in recommending it, and lived to publish several cases, in a postscript to the second edition of his work, in 1767, from which it appears, that scorbutic complaints of the most dangerous kind have actually been cured at sea by the use of wort. Its general effects were, to keep the patients open, and to prove highly nutritious and strengthening. ... As the efficacy of the malt infusion depends upon its producing changes in the whole mass of fluids, it is obvious that it must be taken in large quantities for a considerable length of time, and rather as an article of diet than medicine. The quantity of one to four pints has generally been directed" (113).

Other unusual attempts to grow sprouts on board were recorded by James Lind, in his *Preserving the Health of Seamen*, 1774, giving views expressed as early as 1754 in "A Treatise on the Scurvy." He mentions that one may grow watercress in the hold of a ship by "scattering the seeds over wet cotton or scattering them on blankets soaked in rain water." He records that the Dutch had vegetable gardens on the East India Company's *Sparendam*, in 1670, but that these were frequently washed overboard, and that maintaining gardens ashore on their routes to the Indies, on their colonies on the Cape, was a much better solution (3).

These attempts were abandoned in 1796, when the juice of lemons (which were then called "limes," hence the nickname of the British sailor, "limey," and the name "limehouses" for the waterfront warehouses where the lemons were stored) was adopted as the official antiscorbutic of the British Navy.

The surprising thing about sprouts is how often they are independently "discovered" and exploited when the need is present. An Englishman named Young had reported on the use of sprouted seeds in India as a cure for various diseases within the twenty-year period between Cook's voyage and the adoption of lemon juice in 1796; his observation, which he did not attempt to explain with elaborate theories, was simply that the greatest protection comes from "not dead and dried, but fresh vegetable diet, greens or roots, in sufficient quantity" (146). His remarks so impressed an Edinburgh physician. C. Curtis, that he published a slim volume in 1807, "An account of the Diseases of India as they appeared in the English fleet," which represents less circuitous reasoning than MacBride's, and expands the possibilities for sprouts considerably, since he includes "beans, peas, and other seeds" as possible sources of protection. Perhaps remembering the Dutch experiments, he concedes, "To be sure, we cannot have a kitchen garden at sea, and a short and scanty crop of greens can only be raised aboard ship: but beans, and peas, and barley, and other seeds can be carried in any quantity; and as Mr. Young has very justly stated any kind of esculent seeds brought under the malting or vegetating process, are converted into the state of a growing plant with the vital principle in full activity throughout the germ and pulp; and if eaten in this state without any sort of preparation, except that of separating or rejecting the husks, cannot fail to supply what is wanted for the cure of scurvy, viz., fresh vegetable chyle [emulsified, partially digested food]" (146). He goes on to write, "the malting process is to be performed in shallow frames of wood, constructed so as to preserve the water for successive operations; and a little experience will readily lead to the proper degree of heat and moisture for conducting it successfully." (It is curious that sprouts should generate so much enthusiasm on the part of their discoverers that many of them devise elaborate schemes for growing them in quantity under peculiar or difficult circumstances; the most ingenious example of this will be discussed later.)

During the nineteenth century other antiscorbutics were utilized in the West more widely than sprouts. Beer brewed from malt continued to be considered a primary prophylactic even after 1845, when "improvements" in the malting process, namely kilning the malt at a high temperature, unwittingly led to the destruction of the antiscorbutic vitamin; belief in the powers of beer died hard, however, and Arctic expeditions as late as 1898 still carried malt, yeast and brewing apparatus. In the West sprouts had not yet been used as an article of food but only as a medicine or raw material in alcoholic beverages.

Eastern peoples, of course, had long since recognized the value of sprouted seeds in the ordinary diet, and long-standing traditional use began to be reported during this time by early European explorers and anthropologists. The opening of China and consequent interest in every aspect of Chinese culture had produced a number of articles on diet and cooking, and sprouts, especially of the soybean (then unknown to Europeans), began to be recorded as a major foodstuff. Early missionaries recorded the growing of sprouts in quantity, their sale in the markets as a very popular vegetable (120) and their widespread use in the diet. Sprouted seeds were well-documented by the Dutch as a common foodstuff in the Dutch East Indies (now Indonesia), especially mung bean sprouts, which were called *togé* and were used and relished everywhere. The traditional dishes of Indonesia and the Philippines, built around the rice-table [midday meal] include a vegetable soup, *sayor*, which contains sprouts; a mixed-vegetable platter with peanut-coconut sauce, *gado-gado*, of which *togé* is the main ingredient; several salads that employ steamed *togé;* and a rice and vegetable stew with a fruit-fish sauce, *ketjambah kedelé*, made with soybean sprouts (103). Other seeds were used when mung-beans were unavailable, and a highly valued vegetable, *togé djawa*, was made by using *togé* after just one day's germination, when the root was still very small. One frequently made a stew of *togé*, dried fish and coconut or cooked the sprouts whole (108). Sprouts are recorded as articles of diet in Korea (83), Japan (62, 18) and India (68, 105), where traditional recipes frequently include sprouts. Indian practice called for their use in curries, where they were cooked with rice, coconut, spices and onions, and served with a sauce of cashew nuts, raisins, spices and rosewater (74). Many varieties of legumes completely unfamiliar in this country were used. (The fact that sprouting was such a familiar practice for the Indian soldier was to prove valuable again and again in famines and scurvy epidemics associated with World War I and later.)

Navajo and Zuñi Indians in what are now the states of Arizona and New Mexico in the United States, used sprouted corn in the preparation of an alcoholic beverage, as did many primitive people; they seem to be the only examples of New World peoples who also used sprouted grain in the diet. After the introduction of wheat by the Spaniards, records of both sprouted wheat pudding, *hé palokia,* and a flat sprouted wheat-corn bread appear in anthropological documents (27, 123). Contemporary Zuñi and Navajo still make these traditional dishes in a modernized form.

World War I brought the horror of modern warfare to Western man, but the diseases accompanying it had a familiar sound. Scurvy was probably one of the decisive factors forcing the British surrender in Kut-el-Amara in Mesopotamia in 1916. Special scurvy hospitals were established in Baghdad, Amora and Basra in June of that year (64); and the Lister Institute in London began an exhaustive search for an antiscorbutic that was suited for transport, was easily produced and did not deteriorate under severe climatic conditions. Investigations focused on a beer brewed in South Africa, which used sprouted millet, and sprouted lentils and cowpeas, both used extensively in the diet of the Indian soldier. Material published after the war indicates that these were found to have good antiscorbutic power (36, 43, 54), but it appears that they were never exploited on a large scale by the government.

The only well-documented case of the exploitation of sprouted seeds as an antiscorbutic during World War I comes from an unusual report published by a British army doctor, Major H. W. Wiltshire. He had experimented with antiscorbutics in the Serbian scurvy hospital of which he was the chief medical officer in 1917. He divided sixty of his scorbutic cases into two groups; one group received the traditional antiscorbutic, four ounces of fresh lemon juice, squeezed immediately before use in the ward; the other group ate four ounces of germinated haricot beans that had been boiled for ten minutes. They had been sprouted in "old ration biscuit tins cut in half longitudinally and freely perforated with holes." After four weeks only 53.4 percent of the lemon juice cases were recovered, but 70.4 percent of the sprout cases were pronounced well. The beans were also given to twenty-one cases that had failed to respond to treatment after four weeks; all showed accelerated progress on beans. The Serbs regarded the beans as pig food, which "necessitated frequent explanations of their function." Major Wiltshire concluded his discussion with a long discourse on army cooking methods and how sprouts could be grown in the trenches under fire, with calculations of the amount of space required, the proper temperature and the volume of beans needed to feed a whole battalion. He remarks, "even if no allowance is made for the food value of the beans, the cost of the vitamins supplied by them would still be only 60 percent of the cost when supplied by lemons." The article, which must be among the most remarkable and imaginative medical studies ever published, closes by recommending sprouted seeds as the "easiest and cheapest method" to prevent scurvy in the field (137).

In Karachi, lentils were sprouted in moist blankets and fed to soldiers for their antiscorbutic powers, where they played a major role in the preservation of the health of the Indian troops (59). In 1932 vitamin C was identified and synthesized. Scurvy, one would think, would have been relegated to the status of an historical curiosity. Such was not to be the case, however, for in areas where famines and habitual poverty occur chronically, scurvy continued to be found. Crop failures in the Punjab area of India in 1938 were especially acute. In February, 1940, germinated grain was introduced as a prophylactic against scurvy. Biweekly issues of one ounce of dry grain to each of 200,000 individuals were maintained for four months. Within one month, there were 1,275 fewer deaths than in the same month the previous year; only sixty cases of scurvy were discovered and treated. By March the number was down to nine, and none were found in April. The success of the experiment was so pronounced, however, that the measures were progressively reduced through the summer. By September, 1,002 more deaths had occurred than were reported for the previous September. No germinated grain was given in October, November or December. In January 1941, gratuitous relief was reintroduced for 140,000 people, and scurvy cases again dropped to nil (77). Please note that this does not represent a seasonal rhythm, and that the unusual response of the disease to treatment is perfectly in harmony with observations about it for centuries. Sailors in the final stages of scurvy, so weak they had to be carried ashore, were completely recovered in four to seven days when given fresh fruits and vegetables *ad libitum* (146). Even the small amount provided, one ounce of wheat, millet or gram twice a week, was highly effective as a preventive measure. A health

worker in the area during the third year of the
famine commented, "Germinated grain has much
to commend it as a preventive against food deficiency conditions. Grain in some shape or form is
available everywhere, and the procedure for producing germination is simple. The people are already familiar with grain in this form, as it is par-
taken of at certain festivals, and it does not offend
religious susceptibilities. It contains vitamins A
and B, and particularly C in abundance, and small
quantities added to an otherwise defective diet
make good what is lacking" (101).

During World War II germinated grains were
suggested as possible antiscorbutics by the Minis-
try of Health in Britain in their emergency proce-
dures to deal with the shortage of citrus fruits which
was a result of the blockade of the English merchant
marine. Rose hips, wild fruits, hops and fresh vegetables, however, were emphasized because of their
familiarity. In the United States, the Emergency
Food Commission prepared for a massive protein
shortage, which they calculated would occur some-
time in 1944. One of the earliest alternative protein
sources suggested was sprouted soybeans, largely
due to the efforts and research of Dr. Clive McCay
and his students at the School of Nutrition at
Cornell University. By 1943 a large campaign
was under way to educate the public in the
technique of sprouting soybeans and incorporating
them into the diet. Governor Dewey of New York
gave a luncheon at which was served an entire
menu of dishes made from soybeans, soy flour, and
soy sprouts. *Life* magazine ran a story on the
luncheon in the July 19, 1943 issue, lavishly illus-
trated with pictures of the diners, soybean sprouts
and dishes made from sprouts. Recipes for the

dishes were reprinted; several of these may be found in the recipe section of this book. During the next twelve months agricultural extension services of many universities published free booklets on sprouting (126, 52, 16, 128), and popular family-type magazines and nontechnical journals leaped onto the bandwagon with enthusiastic päeans to the high protein and vitamin content of sprouts, their incredible ease of preparation and their delightful flavor. *Popular Science* called theirs "Victory garden in a flowerpot"; *Better Homes and Gardens* advised one to have a "Kitchen-garden with soybeans"; *Popular Mechanics* said, "Plant beans Monday, eat 'em Thursday." *The New York Times* published recipes for casseroles with soybeans; and even the *Reader's Digest,* a monthly compendium of articles condensed from other magazines, dutifully acknowledged the trend with its own "Are you neglecting the wonder bean?" The U.S. Department of Agriculture issued leaflets, the New York Botanical Garden's Journal and the Oklahoma Academy of Science had their own versions, and *Science Newsletter,* a semi-technical journal, published two articles, emphasizing the necessity for recently harvested soybeans and their value as a meat substitute. The low-calorie aspect of sprouts was emphasized in an article in *Nature Magazine* called "First Aid to Diets."

Dr. Clive McCay and others had also begun sprouting soybeans by the bushel and selling them in the co-op food store in Ithaca, and the extension teachers all over the state taught groups to sprout beans at home. The Emergency Food Commission had published its own booklet, which was available to anyone who wrote to the War Information Service in Albany, New York (79).

The anticipated protein shortage never occurred, however, and by 1945 sprouted soybeans were forgotten by most people, or at least deliberately put aside as were most reminders of the days of food shortages and ration books.

At this time attention was focused on the use of sprouted soybeans and grains for the feeding of domestic animals, especially chickens. The results of many experiments on the effect of supplements of this type on digestibility, egg production and growth rates are highly contradictory, perhaps because of the number of variables involved. The high alpha-amylase content of sprouted grains appears to favorably affect digestion in sheep (81), especially if the sheep have been overfed with protein-rich concentrates, a practice so uneconomical that it is probably rarely encountered. When sprouted soybeans replaced either mash or grain in emergency feeding of chickens, the results were very satisfactory, but no cost comparisons were included to indicate whether this practice was economically beneficial (106). Raw sprouts were found to be less effective in promoting growth in baby chicks than heated beans, for reasons explained later; the amino acid patterns of sprouted soybeans are better adapted to the needs of mammals than to those of birds (90). No data was included on heated germinated soybeans in the diet. A more recent study, which did not include feeding trials on experimental animals but used only chemical analysis of the changes encountered during germination, enthusiastically recommended sprouted soybeans as having "possibilities for use in high-energy, high-protein broiler feed" (91). I am skeptical about such results being economically feasible or realistic from the point of view of time consumed in preparation if the animals are supplied with fresh vegetables, high-quality hay or free-range scratching area.

Experiments using sprouted oats with "shy breeders," cows who failed to conceive after repeated servicing even though apparently functional, are equally difficult to evaluate. Usually, control animals were not carefully regulated or the complete diet of the experimental animals was not reported; and the large cost of purchasing the equipment to produce sprouts, usually in mechanized hydroponic tables, is never included in judging the efficiency of such a method. A comprehensive review of the literature pertaining to the value of sprouting cereal grains for livestock feed concludes that there was no marked effect upon the reproductive function of either heifers or bulls as measured by services required for conception (125).

The nutritional advantages of sprouts seem much higher for humans than for cattle, swine or chickens for several reasons. These animals synthesize their own vitamin C; man and the guinea pig are the only animals that do not. The exchange of energy (calories in the form of carbohydrates) for vitamin C is thus a valueless one for domestic animals. Further, if these animals are receiving fresh food *ad libitum* on pasture, as cut hay or as silage, sprouted oats are contraindicated, for the exchange of carbohydrate for fresh food is even more pointless. Sprouted grains can be recommended only when winter places these feeds at a premium, and it is doubtful whether the cost of producing this food in bulk hydroponically would be matched by increases in growth, fertility or milk production.

Humans are something else again. Recently the use of sprouts as medicine for humans (either a preventive one, as the alternative protein wartime emphasis, or a curative one, as in the case of scurvy) in the West has been superseded by the use of sprouts as food, as they have been in the East. In the early fifties sprouts were grown almost exclusively as Oriental food products, and articles dealing with the difficulties of growing sprouts in bulk for the trade dominate the literature (78). One exception is the appearance of an article in *Organic Gardening*, a relatively obscure journal then, encouraging sprouting soybeans in the home. This journal and others like it nurtured a small flame that has grown in twenty years to a huge blaze of interest in organic foods, their preparation and production. Lawmakers may differ over the definition of "organic" and attempt to stem the flow of new "organic" foods and stores, but many people, first alarmed by Rachel Carson's *Silent Spring* and other books like it, know that for them "organic" means pure, uncontaminated food. Sprouts, now finally embraced in the West as a food in themselves, ironically continue for some to function as a preventive medicine.

Persons seeking an unadulterated source of vegetable matter often view sprouted seeds as an ideal solution. They are in full control of the growing process, and can maintain a purity unobtainable in vegetables grown in soil. If the seeds are guaranteed to be "organically grown," which may mean, ideally, grown in composted soil without the use of chemical fertilizers or poison sprays, they may have a lower residue of chlorinated hydrocarbons than other vegetables. Thus the revival of interest in sprouts in the United States especially, where only DDT is banned, may reflect growing concern over the cumulative effects of persistent pesticides. Sprouts can provide a pure food as well as a highly nutritious one.

CHAPTER THREE

HOW DOES IT HAPPEN?
THE BIOCHEMISTRY OF SPROUTING

Seeds in their dormant state are hard, dry bundles of starch surrounding a tiny embryo. Their metabolism, for they are alive, is so slow as to be almost unmeasurable; their respiration is minute. In this state, seeds can remain for years and still be viable (able to sprout when given the proper conditions). Tests on some legumes show that they can germinate after 200 years of storage under favorable conditions. (I should pause here to note, somewhat regretfully, that the stories of viable wheat seeds taken from Egyptian pyramids are all false. Wheat is quite short-lived, and all seeds from ancient tombs have been found to be entirely broken down to carbon husks) (145). The oldest viable seeds on record were found in a lemming burrow deeply buried in permanently frozen silt of the Pleistocene age in unglaciated central Yukon. They turned out to be a legume, the arctic tundra lupine, and, when taken to the laboratory, they germinated and produced healthy plants. Carbon dating of skulls and other objects found near them in the burrow established their age at at least 10,000 years. Probably only the frozen conditions kept them viable all that time (107).

Yet the question of what kept them alive is not nearly as difficult to answer as the question of what kept them from sprouting at all during those centuries. Dormancy is still a puzzle to plant biochemists. Is it a quiescent period that requires a triggering action to break its sleep? Or is there an actual *block* to growth that must be removed before vital processes can take place? Are dormant seeds sleeping beauties waiting for a prince's kiss or Gullivers tied down while they strain to escape?

If we leave the dynamics out of it, however, dormancy is easy to explain from the evolutionary point of view. It is the seed's way of waiting out a period when conditions are unfavorable to the growth of the new plant. It may wait several seasons until the weather is just right, or, in the case of desert plants, years, until sufficient rain falls to ensure the seedling's survival. In this particular case, germination-inhibiting substances in the seeds may require at least an inch of rain to leach away their restricting action; otherwise, premature sprouting after a light shower, which is quickly evaporated, could be fatal (134). Many seeds, (and, as gardeners know, some early spring blooming bulbs) require a period of cold weather to start them growing again, or even a hard frost to crack the seed coat. Apple seeds rarely if ever germinate within the apple; a cyanide-releasing compound, which is found in the seeds of peaches, pears, apricots, plums and roses, may function as a germination inhibitor. (It does inhibit the germination of other seeds when they are treated with it prior to sprouting). If the apple rots, or passes through the gut of a horse, these substances are washed away, and the seed can germinate (145). Most seeds with which we are familiar are of the cultivated, garden variety; these have been bred to germinate easily. The vast majority of seeds in the wild, however, employ these elegant and complex protective devices to ensure that they will begin life as a plant under the most favorable conditions possible.

Seeds that are sprouted for food are almost all from two highly cultivated families, the *Leguminoseae* (beans, peas, alfalfa) and the *Gramineae* (grasses: wheat, rye, oats, barley), both of which have been domesticated, and consequently bred, for centuries. The Leguminoseae have hard seed coats, but these are easily permeated by water. Sprouting in the home, then, luckily requires no involved process of nicking seeds with a knife, freezing and thawing them, or special aging. One begins with what is considered the first step in the actual germination process: soaking the seeds so that they can take up water into their tissues. During this period of eight to twelve hours, referred to as the "imbibation phase," the dry seeds double or triple in size. But more important, enzymes in the seeds are activated, and begin the complicated series of changes that will result in a new plant. The same enzymes which, in the mouth, degrade starches into sugars and begin the process of digestion, show an intense increase. The dry weight of the seed is decreased as energy is used up. These changes will continue until the new leaves finally appear, on the fourth or fifth day.

After the seeds have imbibed, the water in which they are standing is found to be rich in amino acids, some natural sugars and a large number of inorganic elements. These substances have leached out into the water; under natural conditions, they would return to the soil surrounding the seed when rains and moisture in the soil dissolved them out of the seeds.

The optimum air temperature for rapid sprout

growth appears to be between 25-35° Centigrade (77-95° Fahrenheit). As the temperature becomes lower, sprouting will take place at an increasingly slower rate. Sprouts of seeds that characteristically germinate under very low temperatures, like winter wheat, seem to be higher in ascorbic acid (vitamin C) content than those that germinate under warmer conditions (e.g., spring wheat). Frost-resistant varieties contain even more vitamin C; wheat germinated at 5-8°C. (41-46°F.) contains two to three times that found in wheat germinated at 18-22° C. (65-72° F.) (129). In humans, vitamin C helps prevent capillary fragility (easily broken blood vessels); it is possible that similar action in growing plant tissue could help a plant resist the expansion-contraction effect of freezing and thawing.

Sprouts will continue to grow under severe conditions; their requirements of moisture, air and a favorable temperature range are not narrowly limited, but quite adaptable to a large variety of situations. Yet the elaborate chemical changes that accompany germination are intricate, simultaneous and interrelated metabolic reactions: storage protein is hydrolyzed (broken down into its component amino acids); many vitamins, especially the water-soluble B-complex and vitamin C, are synthesized; fats and carbohydrates are degraded into simple sugars; and some food energy, in the form of calories, is lost. These processes have been intensely studied from the point of view of the use of seeds as a source of human food; the following discussion will view these changes from a similar standpoint.

The intense rise in metabolic activity in a seed that is beginning to germinate is responsible for the phenomenal increase of the water-soluble vitamins; vitamin C and most of the B-complex factor are found in almost all growing plant tissues, and the more active the growth, the higher the concentration of these vitamins. They are essential in the formation of certain enzymes, and therefore vital in cell metabolism. Since sprouting seeds are highly active, increasing to several times their original size in a few days, one might expect to find in them a rich source of vitamins.

Much of the research on vitamin incrementation in germinating seeds as a source of human food has been done in the past two decades by a group of Indian investigators. Faced with staggering nutritional as well as caloric deficiencies, Indian researchers have explored this source, but so far the government has not attempted to exploit sprouting on a major scale. Dr. Sachchidananda Banerjee and others have investigated nearly all of the B-vitamin complex now identified and isolated, and they report rises in every one except folic acid in the germinating seeds of peas (*Pisum sativum*), mung beans (*Phaseolus aureus*), rice, wheat, Bengal gram (*Dolichos lablab*), lentils, horse gram (*Dolichos biflorus*), gram or chick-peas (*Cicer arietinum*), Kalai (*Phaseolus mungo*), barley, cowgram or black-eyed peas (*Vigna catiang*), and kidney or haricot beans (*Phaseolus vulgaris*) (11, 12, 13, 14, 29, 30, 31, 32, 71, 94, 96, 97, 98, 115).

In the early 1940s the United States Army had sponsored investigations in sprouted seeds, hoping to establish their suitability for military use; they found similar rises in the B-vitamin contents of peas, soybeans, navy beans, kidney beans, pinto beans and lima beans (54). These investigations were based on earlier work by Paul Burkholder and

Ilda McVeigh on wheat, barley, corn, oats, soybeans, mung beans, lima beans and peas (23-25). All of these investigators found significant increases in B vitamins and usually waxed enthusiastic over the prospect of incorporating sprouts into the diet. Dr. Burkholder concluded, "If the food value of germinated seeds is to be judged by their content of vitamins and readily available amino acids, then it appears that the common use of sprouts in the diets of Oriental peoples rests on a sound nutritional basis and should be introduced on a wide scale among Occidentals" (24).

Peaks of the various B-vitamins seem to occur at different stages of the germinating process. Thiamine, vitamin B_1, which was originally known as the antiberiberi vitamin, shows a maximum value at 120 hours in lentils and Kalai (an Indian pulse known as urd or black gram), but peaks at 48 hours in black-eyed peas and chick-peas (71). Increases are not nearly as spectacular as in some of the other B-vitamins, however, and agreement on them not nearly as universally held, with some investigators finding no appreciable change in the thiamine content during the first four days, the stage at which consumption is recommended (54), others recording small increases, especially in the grains (23); and others, apparently using a different method of bioassay, reporting increases from 400 to 2,000 percent in thiamine content after five days of germination (71).

After the appearance of leaves and the changeover from stored energy to photosynthesis, thiamine increases greatly, and the last-mentioned figures could possibly be explained in this way. Feeding experiments attempting to find a cure for beriberi or polyneuritis, as it was called at the time of these experiments, show that sprouts may be a good source of vitamin B_1; pigeons with severe beriberi were cured on a ration of one and one-half grams of sprouted mung beans daily (63). Another feeding experiment found that one-half gram of the dried sprout maintained the weight of experimental animals, but one gram of dried beans was ineffective in prevention (116).

Riboflavin, or vitamin B_2, which is considered the growth promoting factor of the B-vitamins, is universally reported as increasing markedly in all parts of the seedling, especially when grown in the dark. Riboflavin is the only B-vitamin destroyed by the presence of light, but it is continually synthesized in seedling, and thus even seeds germinated in direct sunlight contain more B_2 than dormant seeds do (96). Under natural conditions, of course, seeds sprout in the ground or under some sort of cover; normally, they are not exposed to light until the cotyledon pushes the leaves above the surface of the earth, when photosynthesis begins. Most researchers report increases of at least 100 percent in B_2 during this stage; several find much greater increments (130, 96, 23, 24, 33, 97). Methods of storing and handling of foodstuffs that can be a reliable source of this vitamin may ignore its light-sensitivity; milk that is bottled in clear glass may lose most of its B_2 with only a few hours' exposure to sunlight (39). The interdependency of the B-complex makes it important to have a good source of every one of them, and sprouted seeds are an excellent source of this especially elusive one.

Niacin, or nicotinic acid, the pellagra-preventing vitamin, also increases markedly during germination. Pulses (leguminous seeds) contain approximately three times the original amount of niacin in the seed after four days of germination (12). Whole wheat grains are rich in the entire B-complex group; their niacin content almost doubles with germination (23).

It is suspected that the entire B-complex has yet to be isolated and identified; nine factors in addition to the three well-studied ones above have been isolated and named, but experimental animals do not thrive on synthetic diets that contain only the identified vitamins. (Perhaps this is the strongest argument against depending entirely upon the use of synthetic vitamin pills, which may be incomplete in these unknown substances, and an equally compelling reason for choosing a variety of natural food sources of vitamins. The unknown substances probably occur as part of the growth process, even though they are unknown, unnamed and unsung in the literature.) Pantothenic acid, para-aminobenzoic acid, pyridoxine (B_6), choline, inositol, biotin, orotic acid and vitamin B_{12} are all found in germinating seeds, and although the increases are by no means equal, all show some rises as a result of germination. The reports on folic acid are mixed; one researcher reports an increase (23) and another a decrease (14). Substantial increases in biotin, choline, inositol, and pantothenic acid are well-documented (13, 30, 57, 23, 24, 33).

Vitamin B_{12}, of which milk is one of the few good sources, increases in germinating seeds (115); one serving of sprouts provides the amount needed daily. Leafy vegetables contain no B_{12} unless grown on manured soil. Yeast, wheat germ and soybeans contain traces (40). Many vegetarians who eliminate eggs and milk from the diet may suffer from a dangerous-and-difficult-to-recognize deficiency of B_{12}, especially when masked by an abundance of folic acid, usually richly supplied in vegetarian diets. Studies now going on in Great Britain on multi-generation vegetarians may indicate an imbalance of the B-complex that could be irreversibly dangerous. In our country, the sale of folic acid tablets has recently been severely restricted by federal law. Work done so far on the folic-acid-B_{12} ratio of sprouts points to a much more favorable balance for vegetarians than most other foods contain. More research in this area is urgently needed.

The vitamin C content of sprouted seeds has been demonstrated by their historical context; long before vitamin C was identified and isolated, the antiscorbutic qualities of malt and sprouted beans were being exploited in many parts of the world—in times of famine and on long ocean voyages. The recent controversy over the use of massive doses of vitamin C as a cure for the common cold has refocused attention on this vitamin, but it is not my intention to enter this fray, since the amount of vitamin C that one can consume in a single reasonable serving of sprouted seeds does not approach megavitamin treatment. However, this reasonable serving of sprouts provides approximately the recommended adult daily requirement of vitamin C—70 milligrams. (U. S. National Research Council). One-third of that amount has been shown to effectively prevent scurvy in man (45).

Vitamin C is an unusually unstable vitamin; it is destroyed by prolonged exposure to boiling temperatures, by the presence of oxygen, by contact with copper and by oxidation within fruits caused by always-present enzymes. Potatoes, which are a fair source of vitamin C when first dug, lose a good part of this vitamin after ten days; spinach loses as much as 80 percent after two days' storage at room temperature (117). Enzymes, which synthesize vitamins when the plant is growing, are responsible for these losses. When the fruit, leaf or tuber is separated from the plant, other enzymes use up the vitamins until they are gone. In the case of sprouts, which are still growing, live, whole plants when they are used, vitamins are being produced until the moment they are cooked. What a difference from a vegetable that may have been picked one day, packed the next, shipped long distances, wrapped in the shop and then allowed to sit in the vegetable department until it is finally purchased by you to take home, where it may wait further before being cooked and eaten. *All this time* enzymes are breaking down valuable vitamins, especially the unstable vitamin C.

Since the vitamin C formed in sprouts is present when they are eaten, they are a rich source of this vitamin, even after some cooking. A small percentage of vitamin C is destroyed at boiling or steaming temperatures, and some of it is leached out into the cooking water because it is water-soluble; but these losses can be minimized with proper cooking methods. These methods will be discussed in detail in the chapter of recipes.

The initial vitamin increment during germination is so pronounced, however, that sprouted seeds have been used in studies of vitamin C formation pathways. The mechanism is enzymatic in nature and takes place at the expense of sugar (117). Legumes are generally better sources than grains. Whether the increment is measured by chemical methods or by feeding trials on guinea pigs, the vitamin C content of sprouted seeds is remarkable;

100 grams of mung beans (about 3½ ounces), when sprouted, contain 120 milligrams of vitamin C (121). The same weight of Bengal gram or chick-peas yields 75 milligrams. (75). The vitamin content of these legume sprouts compares favorably with orange juice, tomatoes and lemon juice as a source of vitamin C; sprouts yield 180 units (milligrams) per pound, while these fruits contain 150 to 300 units per pound (93). Lemon juice, historically the most commonly used antiscorbutic, contains 0.4 milligram of vitamin C per gram of fresh juice; the same amount of sprouted peas contains 0.9 milligram of vitamin C; and of sprouted mung beans, 1.03 milligrams (87). The average vitamin C content of soybeans rises from 20 to 100 micrograms per soybean in 72 hours of germination (130). Three-day-old seedlings of some oleiferous brassicas (cabbage family) cultivated in Pakistan show a rise from 11 to 15 milligrams of vitamin C in the seeds to 90 to 140 milligrams per 100 grams of sprouts (127). The vitamin C increment is even greater with seeds germinated in the light than in the dark (84), but a corresponding decrease in riboflavin (vitamin B_2) should be expected with seeds grown in the light. Etiolated (grown in the dark) sprouts are generally used by Oriental restaurants; they are considered to be more aesthetically pleasing than green ones, which contain chlorophyll and a larger amount of vitamin C. Commercially grown sprouts are also often bleached with sodium hypochlorite to make them even whiter and to prevent the growth of mold, a practice that does nothing to improve the nutritional value.

Germination in any seed is always accompanied by an intense enzymatic hydrolysis of protein. This means that stored proteins are broken down into their component amino acids, just as they are when the body digests them. This explains why sprouts are more easily assimilated and less gas-forming than dried beans; they are already partly digested. On the average, digestibility doubles with sprouting (2).

Amino acids increase in number (on a dry weight basis) as germination continues (109) at the expense of carbohydrates and fats (102) as the plant synthesizes proteins appropriate to its new needs. The whole process takes place because the protein needs of a seedling are different from those of a seed. Reserve proteins, stored by the seed for just this event in its life, are broken down. One might compare this situation with a complicated house of cards, which is demolished so the cards will be available to construct an entirely different but equally complex house. The blueprint for the new house is called DNA; the builder is called Messenger RNA. The plant is capable of making both blueprint and builder all by itself (19, 28, 37, 53, 58, 89, 104, 109).

The biological value of sprouted seeds, which is measured by the weight gained as a proportion of the total weight of sprouts eaten, surpasses the biological value of seeds in every case. The reason for this may be that the composition (i.e., relative balance) of the amino acid pattern changes little (44), but essential amino acids increase in value at the expense of nonessential ones (19). All amino acid values go up, increasing both in number and in concentration (98). Total protein content of sprouted seeds, then, rises significantly during germination. Mung beans contain 25.07 percent protein, but sprouted mung beans contain 37.30 percent (on a dry weight basis); yellow soybeans increase from 42.99 percent protein in dry seeds to 50.26 percent in sprouts (48).

For centuries it has been observed that heating improved the value of legume seeds, but only recently has the limiting factor been isolated. A heat-labile trypsin or proteolytic inhibitor, which interferes with the utilization of protein, is present in all raw beans and peas. Why beans and peas should manufacture this substance is not known; it may act as a natural preservative during the drying process. Cooking for as little as five minutes destroys 95 percent of the trypsin inhibitor (85), and this improves digestibility and biological values for legumes (132). The trypsin inhibitor retards the very hydrolysis (digestion of protein) that germination begins; thus, germinated raw beans have a higher biological value than ungerminated raw beans (32). This explains why the nutritive value of raw germinated soybeans is higher than that of raw meal, even though the trypsin factor is unchanged. Cooking germinated legumes additionally improves their values; the efficiency (i.e., percent of protein absorbed) of protein in cooked germinated legumes rates higher than that of raw seeds, raw sprouts or cooked seeds (51). The value of an amino acid pattern may be judged by comparing it with egg protein, the most useful for humans; if eggs rate 100 (gain in weight per gram of protein consumed), raw soybeans rate 39, cooked soybeans rate 68 and cooked sprouted soybeans rate 75 (35). Heating also makes the limiting amino acid in legumes, methionine, more available (44). Grains do not contain the trypsin inhibitor; it is therefore not as important to cook them before eating.

The proteins of all grains and legumes are incomplete in some ways, although soybeans and whole wheat are nearly as good as meat (50); for a thorough discussion of protein completeness and supplementation, see Frances Moore Lappé's *Diet for a Small Planet*, published by Ballantine.

Germination is also characterized by a decrease in the dry weight of the seed. (The swelling of the seed due to imbibition makes it weigh a great deal more, of course; the dry weight is what is left after all this water is taken out. Dry weight is the only accurate way to measure real changes, since only then are we making a true comparison of seed with sprout. Even the driest, hardest seed does contain some, but not much, moisture.) The overall loss in dry weight is 20 to 25 percent; this is due to respiratory losses, leakage of soluble materials and the energy loss when the reserve protein and carbohydrate are metabolized (135, 95). Loss in dry weight reflects a loss in caloric content. This is a real gain in any diet, for one exchanges high-calorie fats and carbohydrates for vitamins and protein that are more difficult to find. The carbohydrates are changed to sugars, the same ones found in the fresh fruits and recently picked vegetables that give them their superlative flavor. As the root emerges, the sugar content rises rapidly. By the sixth day, starch is reduced from 30 to 5.4 percent; total sugars rise from 1.5 to 8.3 percent (135). The enzyme responsible for this is alpha-amylase. which is found in the mouth of every human above the age of six months; immediately after the imbibition phase, this enzyme shows a great increase (76). Oils are also depleted, and play an important role in carbohydrate metabolism (1, 67, 46). The free fatty acid percentage of crude fat present in the seed rises (22, 69, 58), even though the total fat content changes very little; the saturated fatty acid content drops after four days (136). The tocopherol content increases during germination (31) and the alpha-tocopherol especially; this last mentioned one is the elusive vitamin E (60). From the point of view of human nutrition, these last two metabolic patterns are extremely fortunate; vitamin E is highly unstable since it is quickly destroyed if exposed to air. Oils and whole grains, refined, hydrogenated and heated to high temperatures in processing, contain little. Saturated fats (butter and animal fats as well as hydrogenated oils and natural coconut and palm kernel oil) seem to be used more widely than unsaturated liquid vegetable oil in our diet; a good balance is half saturated, half unsaturated, but few average diets maintain this. Sprouts provide us with an excellent, yet inexpensive, way to obtain these difficult nutrients.

Sprouting seeds increases their content of carotene (vitamin A precursor) (29); eight legumes and two grains all showed significant rises. The carotene content of dried seeds is not very high to begin with; intensely green vegetables are a better source. In winter, when sprouts are more likely to be used, however, one should exploit every available source. The vitamin K content of germinated seeds, again a minor source, increases steadily and peaks on the sixth day in sprouts grown in the light (49).

Most of the changes that occur on germination, then, are beneficial to humans. The seed's preparations for becoming a plant include quite a few most fortunate patterns. Even though the function of all of these metabolites is unknown, their presence is

well-documented. Just as one can drive an auto-
mobile without being able to explain exactly how it
works, one can exploit these valuable additions to
the vegetable kingdom without knowing exactly
why the plant goes to all this trouble and effort.

CHAPTER FOUR

HOW TO SPROUT AT HOME

Any viable seed will sprout under the proper conditions, but not all sprouts are edible or palatable. Lupine and wisteria seeds, which are in the legume family, are poisonous, as are potato and tomato sprouts. Many spice and herb seeds, like coriander and pepper, will sprout beautifully, but the sprout is so strong-flavored that it is unpalatable, if nourishing. The most successful sprouts for eating come from the *Leguminoseae* (peas, chick-peas, beans, fenugreek, alfalfa or lucerne, clover, lentils and soybeans), *Gramineae* (wheat, rye, corn, barley, millet and oats) and the *Cruciferae* (mustard, radish, cress and kale). A few others from the other families will add variety: parsley, carrots, dill, celery, beets, buckwheat, flax, purslane, lettuce, caraway, onions, sesame and chia. Rice, even brown rice, has had the outer hull removed and will not sprout.

Make sure the seeds are food-quality, untreated with mold retardants, fungicides or insecticides. The best way to purchase seed is from a health food store, because you will be understood if you explain that you intend to use the seeds for sprouting and therefore need viable, untreated seeds. Seeds that fail to sprout should be taken back to the store, as they are probably too old; food values of such seeds drop as their stored food is exhausted, and they are less nourishing than they should be if you soak and boil them without sprouting. Many beans available in shops may be treated with inhibitors, especially to retard sprouting; you will be unable to tell whether age or treatment has spoiled your crop, but you will know that something is wrong if you follow directions carefully and end up with a slimy, evil-smelling mess. It is usually wise not to use seed-quality seeds (i.e., those packed especially for gardeners) for sprouting because they may be treated even if the package is not marked as such and they will certainly be more expensive.

Sprouts of different seeds vary in their taste, texture and length of cooking time. Some sprouts will seem very familiar to you; there is a basic taste common to the legume family that is more pronounced raw than cooked. The brief descriptions of seeds which follow will give you only the vaguest idea of what you can do with each one. Consult the recipe index for recipes under the name of each seed, and then try to devise new combinations that exploit these slightly familiar but nonetheless new tastes.

MUNG BEAN (*Phaseolus radiatus* or *P. aureus*) sprouts, also called green gram, are the most familiar sprouts to beginners; they are used in Chinese restaurants and sold fresh and canned in many food shops. They are crisp and have a delightful flavor, something like raw peas. They are ready to eat when the root is 1½ to 2½ inches long. They cook very quickly, in three minutes or less. It is not necessary to remove either the bean or the green skin, although the skin may be floated off by flooding the sprouts with water immediately before use.

SOYBEAN (*Glycine max*) sprouts are used widely in China and are the nutritional giants of sprouting. They are one of the five sacred grains of prehistoric times; the others are wheat, rice, barley and millet. The Chinese use black, blue and white beans, and the green soybean developed in the U.S. especially for human consumption is very successful. The small yellow soybean, most commonly sold here as a dried bean, is also excellent. They are all considered difficult to sprout because they sometimes develop sour odors, especially in hot weather. You may avoid this by being careful to rinse the sprouts often, and to pick out broken and discolored seeds and seeds that show no life after the first day. Wait until the root is 1½ to 2 inches long before using. Soybean sprouts require ten to fifteen minutes of cooking, but are delicious and higher in protein than any other bean. Beatrice Trum Hunter, in her *Natural Foods Cookbook*, recommends Chief, Ebony, Illini, Lincoln and Richland as the best varieties for sprouts; the United States Department of Agriculture recommends Peking, Cayuga and Otootan because they germinate quickly and uniformly. Food-quality seeds are not usually identified by variety, unfortunately.

LENTILS (*Lens esculenta*), named *Lens* because their shape resembles the lens of a telescope, are vastly improved by sprouting. They become sweeter, more tender and more delicate in flavor, and require only five minutes to cook instead of the thirty commonly needed for soaked, dried lentils. Use when the root is 1 inch long. Split red lentils are not suitable because they are killed when the seed coat is broken; without its protective shell, the bean dries out.

PEAS (*Pisum sativum*), available dried for soup or soaking and cooking as a vegetable, make excellent sprouts; split peas, as discussed above, will not do. The rising sugar content causes the flavor to resemble that of the fresh vegetable much more so than if the peas were merely soaked and boiled. Wrinkled or smooth varieties are equally successful. Use when the root is 2 inches long; simmer five minutes or less.

CHICK-PEAS (*Cicer arietinum*) or *garbanzos* as they are called in Mexico and their native Spain, are the major pulse crop grown in India. There they are called Bengal gram, *chana* or *chhola*. This bean is mealy in texture but delicate in flavor; it is used as a starch in near Eastern cooking as well as in the New World. The sprout is more tender and delicious than the bean, and requires five to eight minutes of cooking. When ready to eat, the root is 1½ to 2 inches long.

ALFALFA OR LUCERNE (*Medicago sativa*) has not been used for sprouting historically, but it has been used widely in recent years as part of the health-food enthusiasm in the United States. Sprouts should be used when the root is 1½ inches long. At this point they will have tiny green leaves, and they should be used immediately, since the appearance of leaves signals a switch within the plant to photosynthesis as a source of energy, and the exhaustion of the stored food in the seed. Alfalfa originated in North Africa, where it is used as a forage crop; it is used as green manure and fodder in the U. S. The sprout does not taste as much like a bean as other legumes do; but the texture is very crisp and delicate, and the tiny, thin sprouts cook almost immediately. Several of the authors of other books on sprouting consider the alfalfa sprout to be the supreme sprout, high in protein, chlorophyll, potassium, vitamin A, vitamin K and calcium, although they may not be able to substantiate these claims.

FENUGREEK (*Trigonella foenum-graecum*) is one legume still widely used in medicine, as well as for food and for teas. The name means "Greek hay" in Latin. This pungent, spicy seed is used in curries, and it makes a slippery, soothing tea. Sprouts of fenugreek seed are best when cooked only a few minutes; long cooking produces a bitter flavor. Use when the sprout is 1 to 1½ inches long. Be sure to buy whole fenugreek seed; the broken seeds are commonly sold for brewing tea.

OTHER LEGUMES that may be sprouted are lima beans (*Phaseolus lunatus*); marrow beans, pinto beans, kidney beans, French or haricot beans, navy beans (*P. vulgaris*); the aduki or adzuki bean (*P. angularis*); black gram or urd (*P. mungo*); sona mung or maskalai (*P. roxburghii*); the broad bean or horse bean (*Vicia faba*); the black-eyed pea, cowgram or *lobia* (*Vigna catiang*); the pigeon pea, red gram or arhar (*Cajanus indicus*); the hyacinth bean or field bean (*Dolichos lablab*); and several others less familiar. Since many of these beans are grown almost exclusively in the Middle and Near East, it might be difficult to buy them here.

WHEAT (*Triticum sativum*) is the most delicious for sprouts of all the grains. It seems to resemble fresh corn just picked, for the starches in the wheat are degraded to the same sugars found in corn. It should be used when the sprout is the same length as the seed, just ½ inch or less; as the root grows longer, it becomes tough and stringy, like the roots of sod. Sprouting in the grains goes along much faster than in the legumes, and they do not slow down as much when chilled, so care should be taken not to allow grains to form a dense, interwoven, tangled mass of long, tough roots. Wheat sprouts are not the same as "wheat grass," which consists of just the leaves, chopped fine, after they have grown several inches. The sprouts cook quickly, in eight minutes or less.

BARLEY (*Hordeum vulgare*) has been studied more thoroughly than any other seed used in sprouting because of its importance in the malting process, the initial step in the brewing of beer. Of course, any grain may be used for malting; but barley converts a larger amount of starch to sugar, and the more sugar available, the more alcohol may be produced. The chemistry of barley sprouting is thus the subject of a good deal of research. Each sugar has been identified and measured, and thus the process may be manipulated according to the desires of the individual brewer. Barley, rye and oats are all similar to wheat in that they should be used when the root is no longer than the seed itself to avoid a sod-like matted mass of roots. All the grains may be eaten raw or sautéed in a little butter or steamed briefly.

CORN is a difficult choice for sprouts since it is almost never found with the germ intact. Lying near the jointure of each individual grain with the cob, it is often removed during shelling and may be damaged enough to be killed even if it looks perfectly sound. Great care should be taken to remove damaged seeds and those not sprouting in the early stages. The roots may be grown 1 inch long. Cook until tender, eight to ten minutes.

CHIA, FLAX, PURSLANE (*Portulaca oleracea*),

and **PSYLLIUM** seeds are all very interesting in that they are mucilaginous seeds and thus laxative; they produce a slippery mass that is quite bulk-forming. For this reason they are very difficult to drain as they hold water and may form a gelatinous ball that will rot. They should be shaken thoroughly after rinsing, or drained on absorbent paper to counteract their very high surface tension. Added to soups they give a gumbo effect, and can be very tasty. Use when the sprout is as long as ½ inch, but no longer. These seeds are very tiny.

A daily diet of **RADISH, CRESS, LETTUCE, MUSTARD, DILL, PARSLEY** or **CELERY** sprouts would be too highly seasoned for the average palate, but these tiny peppery morsels add a great deal to a green salad. Everyone is familiar with the clipped cress added to salad plates, but not everyone knows that, grown in water instead of soil, the root and seed may be eaten too. Chop fine and add to mixed greens, garden vegetables or pickles. Use in stuffed eggs, cheese dishes or as a garnish. Like the grains, these cresses contain no trypsin inhibitors and need not be cooked. Use when the root is ½ to ¾ inch long, as soon as the tiny green leaves appear. For crispness, this group is unrivaled.

A number of utensils may be used for sprouting. It is simpler to use a container with natural drainage than one that requires the transfer of the sprouts from one place to another after rinsing, because they may be spilled or the tender root may be broken off, and they will rot. Treat sprouting seeds gently. Among the various containers with natural drainage are colanders, large strainers, large percolator-type coffeepots (use the basket where one puts the grounds), vegetable baskets, large un-

SPROUTING CONTAINERS

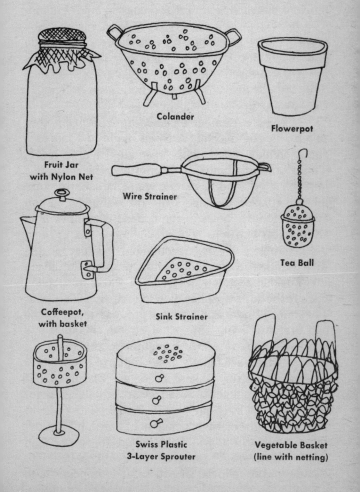

Fruit Jar
with Nylon Net

Colander

Flowerpot

Wire Strainer

Tea Ball

Coffeepot,
with basket

Sink Strainer

Swiss Plastic
3-Layer Sprouter

Vegetable Basket
(line with netting)

glazed flowerpots with net over the hole, ball-type tea strainers (for small seeds), or large fruit jars with nylon net stretched over the top secured with a rubber band. These last are my favorite; for ease, simplicity and visibility, they are excellent. Nylon net or tulle may be purchased very cheaply at any fabric store; a square 6 x 6 inches is large enough for even the largest jar. Nylon will not rot, will not absorb odors from the waste products the seeds create, will not deteriorate for a long time and need not be sterilized after each use, as cheesecloth must. It will discolor, but this makes no difference. Use two thicknesses with tiny seeds.

There are a number of elaborate sprouting containers on the market. A Swiss-made one features three shallow trays with a small drain in each. Three separate kinds of sprouts may be used, one on each level, and the same water is used to rinse all. A variation on this is the three-drawer bureau type, which has holes in the floor of each drawer to allow water to drain.

Sprouters I do not recommend because of the difficulty involved in obtaining proper ventilation are Turkish towels wrung out in water and rolled up, synthetic sponges or blotting paper. These tend to retain off-odors and give a peculiar taste to the sprouts. All living things, of course, make waste products as part of their metabolic processes. In sprouts, these are mostly gases that are removed by rinsing and airing. These gases are harmless, but they can be pungent. Select clean, whole seeds for your crop. Picking out broken seeds, weed seeds or pebbles now will save you much time and energy later, when these will have failed to sprout and must be *carefully* removed to avoid damage to their growing fellows. Of course, it is impossible to tell whether a seed is alive by looking at it; a second inspection will be required later to remove all dead material. Do not be too hasty to discard seeds that show no immediate signs of life, since germination rates may vary considerably. Allow at least thirty-six hours after the first seeds begin to show signs of life before discarding their slower, but perhaps viable, neighbors.

One begins the process by soaking the seeds until they swell to almost double in bulk. This will require two to eight hours, and the seeds may be allowed to "imbibe" (the scientific term) overnight. When the seeds have soaked, the water in which they were standing will show a slight change of color, for it contains some dissolved minerals, free amino acids, and sugars. Don't discard it; use it in cooking, soups or juices. It is practically tasteless.

If you are dismayed because you like to have more specific instructions than "two to eight hours," please don't be. The quality of the sprouts seems to be unaffected by the length of imbibition, nor does this variation seem to change the length of time required for the sprouts to reach maturity. Soybeans, which have peculiar difficulties associated with germination, should be soaked as little as possible, since long soaking may accentuate their tendency to mold, especially if the weather is warm. Warm water shortens the soaking period, but not the total time required for sprouting.

Make sure the jar you use is of an adequate capacity to accommodate all the seeds. Most seeds increase six to eight times in bulk during germination. This means that two ounces of seeds will nearly fill a pint jar when sprouted. It is probably wise to measure three or four tablespoons of seeds into a quart fruit jar to give yourself room for active rinsing. This will make approximately one pint of sprouts, except in the case of very tiny seeds, which will make slightly more. The recipes, which will make four to six portions unless otherwise noted, generally require either one pint, or two cups, of sprouts, if they constitute the main ingredient, or one cup if they are to be combined with other primary ingredients. Some seeds will swell so much during this initial soaking that they will become jammed into a solid layer in the bottom of the jar. This seems to occur more often with chick-peas than with any other seed. Should this occur, *gently* pry the layer apart with a fork or dull knife, remembering that it is easy to damage the seed by piercing or scraping it.

In the next few days, all you need do is rinse the sprouts two or three times each day. The rinsing removes waste gases and keeps the sprouts moist. After each rinsing, drain the sprouts *thoroughly*. If the seeds are permitted to stand in water, they will rot. If they are allowed to dry out, they will shrivel and die.

Many persons who go out to work feel that they cannot grow sprouts because they need attention more frequently than they are home to give it. This is foolish; one can rinse the sprouts at breakfast, when one returns from work and again before bed; they will respond beautifully to this timing. Placing the jar on the sink will make it easy to remember to perform this simple task, when one fills the kettle for tea, begins to prepare dinner or does the washing up.

A marvelous mechanism in the root keeps the seed constantly informed as to which way is down. In the soil, this would insure that the root travels the right way. Have you ever dug up a bulb that had been planted upside down? The root and leaf both know that they must reverse themselves to get started right, and they do, a laborious if necessary project. Your seeds, if left undisturbed, will grow long, straight roots as nearly vertically as they can. If you use a fruit jar, which involves pouring water in the top through the net, draining the jar upside down and then placing the jar on its side, you will change the orientation of the sprouts each time you do this, and the roots will not be long and straight, but curly and twisted. This does not affect the quality of the sprouts at all; in fact, it makes them rather picturesque. The long, straight root of commercial bean sprouts is made by allowing the seeds to remain undisturbed during sprouting (which is done in bulk in huge twenty-gallon drums), and they are rinsed by pouring water over them and allowing it to drain out the bottom. The method you use will determine your sprouts' shape, and this is entirely a matter of personal taste.

Many persons are surprised to learn that sprouted seeds do not require darkness to grow properly. Of course, in their natural condition (under a layer of soil), they would be in the dark, but sprouting in the light appears to be beneficial from the point of view that more chlorophyll and vitamin C are formed than in the dark. In the light, one sacrifices some vitamin B_2 (riboflavin), which is destroyed in the presence of light, but it is also constantly synthesized in the growing plant.

When your sprouts have reached the correct length, you may slow down growth considerably by refrigerating them. They will continue to grow, but if you cannot use them on the day they are ready, they will wait. Do not allow them to dry out or sit in water, just as you would not when they are growing. The optimum temperature for germination is about 80°F., certainly warmer than the average kitchen. A warm spot, free from drafts, is very beneficial. For each 10° cooler, the rate will slow down appreciably. At 60°F., sprouting proceeds very slowly. Grains appear to be less affected than legumes by low temperatures.

If your sprouts sit in water, they will rot and smell dreadful. If they dry up, wither and turn brown, they will die. A few dead seeds will sometimes mold and give an unpleasant odor to the lot; remove these and rinse well. There is no need to discard your living sprouts should this occur. If a large proportion of your seeds fail to sprout, it may be that they were dead when you purchased them. If so, the supplier should be informed that his stock is not fresh. Water which has been highly treated with chemicals could conceivably cause difficulty, but I have never seen a case of this myself.

CHAPTER FIVE

RECIPES

Because of the trypsin factor in raw legumes, beans and peas should be simmered or steamed three minutes or less, just until hot through. Moist heat has been shown to be more effective than dry in destroying this substance. Care should be taken not to cook them overlong, since other valuable amino acids will suffer from overcooking (90). Of course, a few raw sprouts will not affect your digestion seriously any more than a few raw peas you shelled and ate in your garden would give you indigestion. Steaming for three minutes will not make sprouts any less crisp or crunchy than raw ones; they will still have "bite." The water in which you simmered them will contain some vitamin C and natural sugars; it is practically tasteless, and should be saved with soaking water to use in cooking.

Do not add salt, fat or acids to sprouts at the beginning of cooking. Salt attracts water away from the sprout; fat coats the outside and prevents moisture from penetrating the sprout. The acid in molasses or vinegar toughens the outside. Add these after sprouts are tender, if possible.

Palatability experiments conducted on different methods of cooking showed that most people preferred the taste of sprouts that had been "panned" (i.e., stir-fried with one tablespoon of oil and a small amount of water) to those that had been boiled (139). Boiling is more destructive to the vitamin C content than either steaming or panning, and reducing the amount of water reduces the vitamin losses. Soybean sprouts boiled for ten minutes in a large amount of water lose 75 percent of their vitamin C (about three-quarters of this loss represents diffusion into the cooking water, and only one-fourth oxidation (61)), but those steamed fifteen minutes lose only 40-50 percent, and sautéeing in one tablespoon of oil and one-third cup of water for ten minutes results in the loss of only 20-30 percent of the vitamin C (35). The acidity of sprouts acts to protect the vitamin C content: less is lost as a result of oxidation within the plants (93). Freezing six months at 0°F. after blanching results in a loss of 70 percent of the vitamin C (82). Since sprouts are so easy to produce at any time, however, freezing should be unnecessary. Because of vitamin losses during cooking, I recommend adding sprouts as close to the end of the cooking period as possible. Soybean sprouts require ten to fifteen minutes of cooking, but most others will be tender in three to five minutes. Your own taste should be your guide.

Grains and legumes contain amino acids which together form complete proteins, i.e., most like those of eggs, which are the most useful to humans. For a complete and excellent discussion of amino acid supplementation, see Frances Moore Lappé's *Diet for a Small Planet*, published by Ballantine. In devising your own recipes, and in these that follow, please note that for every one-half tablespoon of legumes, dry and unsprouted, four tablespoons of raw dry rice will give the most efficient proportion of amino acids; and for every tablespoon of legumes, five tablespoons of wheat. Soybeans are a slight exception; their ideal proportions to rice are one to ten, and to wheat one to three.

"Stir-frying" is the traditional Oriental method of cooking vegetables and meat. The individual ingredients are cut, sliced or chopped into small pieces, and assembled ready to cook just before the meal is to be served. The pan used, a *wok*, is a shallow metal bowl; a heavy skillet will do just as well. The *wok* is heated with one tablespoon of oil in it. When the oil is very hot, but not smoking, the vegetables are added; the ones that require the longest cooking time are added first, but the entire cooking time is measured in minutes rather than hours. With a large spoon or spatula, the whole mixture is stirred constantly; when the last ingredients are in, a sauce of broth, soy sauce, seasoning and thickening is added. This is just allowed to boil; the vegetables should be at the point described as "tender-crisp" and should retain their original color. Serve at once. This method preserves the maximum number of nutrients: initial heating is rapid, which destroys enzymes that break down vitamins; the food is cooked very quickly, before heat destroys the vitamins; all the vitamins and minerals dissolved out by the cooking water are eaten in the sauce. This method is recommended for every kind of vegetable.

Many of the promotors of sprouts recommend liquified drinks of sprouts in various fruit juices, calling them "vitality cocktails" or "pick-me-up's." Because the sprouts are used raw, I cannot recommend them unless your digestion is excellent. I have included two of these in the soup section, and they may be heated and served as soup if you wish.

A common practice among the traditional users

of sprouted seeds is to remove the cotyledon (bean) and use only the hypocotyl (root or radicle). One group of researchers ascertained the vitamin contents of the seed and root separately, and concluded that the practice is unsound from a nutritional point of view, since the vitamins they assayed (vitamins A, B_1, B_2, niacin and C) are more concentrated in the cotyledon after sprouting in a ratio of three or four to one (130).

Most of the recipes require one or two cups of sprouts, and are designed to serve four to six people. Since seeds expand in volume approximately eightfold during germination, you may wish to remember that two rounded tablespoons (one ounce) of seeds will produce one cup of sprouts, and four rounded tablespoons (two ounces) will produce approximately two cups of sprouts. The smaller the seeds, the greater the increase in volume will be. The measurements given in the recipes are approximate and need not be followed exactly; in fact, I hope you will deviate considerably from them as your enthusiasm and imagination lead you.

Soups and Beverages

Sprouts lend themselves especially well to almost all soups. Any canned or dried soup may be enriched with a handful of mung bean or alfalfa sprouts just before you take it off the stove to serve it. The stored heat cooks the delicate sprouts instantly.

BEAN SPROUT EGG-DROP SOUP

This traditional Chinese soup is an excellent starter to a light meal.

3 c. clear soup, vegetable   2 beaten eggs
    broth, or stock   salt or soy sauce
2 c. soybean sprouts

Heat the soup to boiling and add the sprouts. Simmer until tender, 8 to 10 minutes. Remove from the fire and drizzle into it the beaten eggs off the end of a spoon, slowly so that the eggs cook into soft, fine threads. Season to taste with salt or soy sauce.

CREOLE SOUP

This is nearly a main dish in itself. With grilled cheese on toast, it would make a fine supper.

1 can stewed tomatoes   2 garlic cloves, minced
    (1 lb., 12 oz.)   pinch marjoram and basil
2 c. soybean sprouts   1 t. salt
1 large onion, chopped   ½ t. pepper
                              2 T. sugar

Put everything into a saucepan. Cover and simmer 10 to 15 minutes or until the sprouts are tender.

MINESTRONE PRESTO

2 c. water or stock
1 c. chick-pea sprouts
1 small head cabbage, grated
1 bunch spinach, chopped
1 bunch parsley, chopped
4 carrots, diced

2 c. milk
sherry to taste
8 oz. grated Parmesan cheese
1 clove garlic, minced
olive oil (if desired)

Simmer everything for 15 minutes, or until the sprouts are tender. Do not overcook! A little olive oil is good in this. Serve with Italian bread.

KOREAN BEEF SOUP WITH DUMPLINGS (MAN-TU)

This traditional recipe calls for removing the bean from the sprout and chopping the sprout finely. If you wish to be very authentic, you can do this, but it is a lot of trouble. The beans thus removed are not used in this recipe.

1 lb. beef (round or flank steak)
2 green onions, chopped
2 T. toasted sesame seed
6 T. soy sauce
1½ cloves garlic, chopped
pepper
6 c. water or stock
2 t. oil

1 t. salt
¼ lb. mushrooms, finely chopped
1 c. bean sprouts, steamed and finely chopped
1 c. chopped, cooked celery cabbage
3 c. unbleached flour
1 c. water
3 T. pine nuts (pignolia seeds)
1 egg, beaten and fried

The soup is made as follows: cut ¼ lb. beef into thin slices 1 inch square. Add 1 chopped onion, 1

T. toasted sesame seed, 2 T. soy sauce, ½ clove of chopped garlic and pepper. Mix well. Cook until meat is seared, add 6 c. water or stock, and simmer until tender.

To make the filling, grind ¾ lb. of beef fine. Add to it 1 chopped onion, 1 T. sesame seed, 4 T. soy sauce, 1 chopped clove of garlic, pepper, 2 t. oil, salt, the finely chopped mushrooms, bean sprouts and celery cabbage. Mix well.

To make the dumplings: mix the flour and 1 c. water to make a stiff dough. Knead for 5 minutes; roll into a snake 1 inch in diameter. Cut into 1 inch pieces; roll each piece into a 3 inch circle. Put 1 spoonful of filling on each, add 2 or 3 pine nuts, fold over and seal. Drop into the boiling soup and cook 2 minutes after they come to the top. Decorate with slivers of fried, beaten egg in ½ inch diamond-shaped pieces. Serve at once, 6 per person.

WINTER VEGETABLE SOUP

A hearty soup with lots of vegetables for a cold day.

2 T. *(1 oz.) butter or dripping*	2 *turnips, diced*
2 *onions, grated*	2 *small potatoes, diced*
2 *carrots, finely chopped*	2 *c. consommé or beef stock*
* * *	
2 *c. sprouted peas or lentils*	1 *T. salt*
	½ *t. pepper*

Sauté the onions in butter until golden; add carrots, turnips and potatoes, and stir fry until tender. Add the stock and heat to the boiling point. Add the sprouts, salt and pepper at the last, simmering only until the sprouts are tender. Celery, parsnips or cabbage may be used as alternate or additional vegetables.

LENTIL SOUP

This traditional soup may be served as a purée or not, as you like.

2 c. lentil sprouts
4 c. boiling stock
a piece of ham,
    finely chopped

1 large onion, minced
3 T. butter
pepper

Drop the lentil sprouts into the boiling stock with the ham. Simmer 10 minutes or until tender. Sauté the onion in the butter, add pepper, and combine with the sprouts mixture. Blend in a blender or put through a sieve.

SWEET-AND-SOUR LENTIL OR BLACK BEAN SOUP (Serves 4)

The flavor of this soup will remind you of Chinese soup, but the lentils are, of course, not traditional.

4 c. chicken broth
4 or 5 mushrooms, sliced
    thin
¼ lb. boneless pork,
    sliced thin
1 t. salt
1 T. soy sauce
2 T. vinegar

2 c. lentil or black bean
    sprouts
2 T. cornstarch in 3 T.
    cold water
2 T. brown sugar
¼ t. ground pepper
2 green onions,
    with tops, chopped

In a heavy saucepan, combine the broth, mushrooms, pork, salt, soy sauce and vinegar. Bring to a boil and simmer 3 minutes. Add the bean or lentil sprouts and simmer 8 to 10 minutes, or until tender. At the last minute add the cornstarch mixture, the sugar and pepper, and boil 1 minute, or until clear and thick. Add green onions, and serve at once.

BERNARD JENSEN'S VITALITY COCKTAIL (Serves 1)

1 c. apple juice   *1 t. wheat germ*
½ c. mung bean sprouts   *1 T. sunflower seeds*

Blend in liquifier until of a smooth creamy texture.

BERNARD JENSEN'S SPROUT PICK-ME-UP (Serves 2)

2 c. orange juice   *honey to taste*
2-3 T. tahini (liquified   *1 c. alfalfa sprouts*
* sesame seed)*

Combine the ingredients and blend until well mixed.

SWEETWORT

This brew was prepared by Captain Cook on his voyages of exploration according to the recommendation of Dr. David MacBride. It is not alcoholic but is quite sweet and very nourishing.

2 c. barley sprouts   *honey to taste*
6 c. boiling water

Grind the barley sprouts in a meat grinder, or place in a blender with a third of the water and liquify. Add the rest of the boiling water and allow the brew to stand for several hours or until cool. Strain. A very refreshing beverage, it may be reheated and served with honey to taste. To preserve the antiscorbutic qualities, do not boil.

Salads

A PRIORI SALAD

So named because it was devised by Mary Prior, a friend from Oxford.

1 no. 2½ can (3½ c.)
  corn, drained
1 raw cauliflower, broken
  into flowerets
1 c. mung bean sprouts,
  steamed 3 minutes and
  cooled

2 raw red or green
  peppers, cut into strips
oil and vinegar, salt and
  pepper, mixed for a
  dressing

Lightly toss the vegetables in the oil and vinegar dressing.

NORTH COUNTRY SALAD

Kate Hodgson, a teacher at North Country School, sprouted mung beans for the whole school and served them in this salad. Try serving with tacos and cottage-cheese cake.

1 large apple, chopped
juice of ½ lemon
2 T. light oil
2 T. honey
salt

3 carrots, grated
1 c. mung bean sprouts,
  steamed 3 minutes and
  cooled

To make the dressing, shake in a jar the lemon juice, oil, honey and salt. Toss the vegetables lightly in the dressing.

SALADE OLIVIER

An elegant salad for a dinner party; serves 6 very well.

2 avocado pears, sliced
into 1 inch chunks
½ lb. mushrooms, sliced
1 cucumber, unpeeled,
chopped
juice of 1 lemon
2 small jars marinated
artichoke hearts

olive oil (if needed)
1 c. mung bean sprouts,
steamed 3 minutes
and cooled
2 T. chopped parsley
salt and pepper

Marinate the avocado chunks, raw mushrooms and cucumber in the lemon juice and the oil drained from the artichoke hearts. Add a small amount of olive oil if necessary. Toss with sprouts, chopped parsley, salt and pepper.

POTATO SALAD VIVA

A delicious potato salad with an interesting texture.

1 lb. cooked, peeled,
cubed waxy potatoes
1 onion, grated fine
1 c. mung bean sprouts,
steamed 3 minutes
and cooled
2 stalks celery, diced

½ c. mayonnaise or
salad dressing
1 T. Worcestershire
sauce
1 t. salt
1 bunch parsley,
chopped

Mix all ingredients together and chill well.

BREAKFAST SALAD

From Beatrice Trum Hunter.

2 c. wheat sprouts
1 c. sunflower seeds,
hulled
3 apples with skins,
grated

½ c. raisins
½ c. yogurt
3 bananas, sliced

Lightly toss all ingredients together in serving dish.

SALAD A L'AMERICAINE

As served in the restaurant at the Rural Life Exhibition on the occasion of H. H.'s Diamond Jubilee, 1936.

¼ c. olive oil	2 c. soybean sprouts, steamed 10 minutes
¼ c. vinegar	
1 t. sugar	1 small cabbage, shredded finely
1 t. salt	
pepper	1 c. sour cream

Bring the oil, vinegar, sugar, salt and pepper to a boil; pour over the vegetables. When quite cold, stir in the sour cream.

CRUNCHY SPROUT SALAD

Molded gelatin salads need a great deal of textural variation to raise them from a mundane level to something worth serving. Sprouts do this and add a delightful taste as well.

1 pkg. (or 1 T.) unflavored gelatin	2 T. chopped chives
	½ c. shredded cabbage
4 T. cold water	½ c. grated carrot
2 c. boiling water	½ c. chopped celery
juice and grated rind of 1 lemon	½ c. sprouted mung beans
1 t. salt	

Soak the gelatin in cold water. Dissolve in boiling water. Add lemon juice and rind and salt. Chill. When partly set, add the vegetables and pour into a mold.

URAB (Indonesia)

A very unusual salad, this vegetable-coconut mixture *requires* freshly grated coconut. Do not try to make it with packaged shredded coconut, because the texture will be all wrong.

2 c. fresh mung bean
   sprouts
1 small cabbage, finely
   shredded
1 bunch fresh spinach,
   chopped
2 c. green beans, cut in
   1 inch lengths

5 T. lemon juice
dash hot pepper sauce
pinch powdered ginger
2 t. salt
1 T. soy sauce
1 coconut, shelled and
   coarsely grated

Steam the vegetables, one at a time, until just tender—bean sprouts and cabbage, 5 minutes; spinach, 3 minutes; beans 8 to 10 minutes, depending on their age. Then chill the vegetables. Combine the lemon juice, hot pepper sauce, ginger, salt and soy sauce, and mix well. Drop the coconut into this dressing and toss until well covered. Mix with the chilled vegetables just before serving.

ASINAN (West Java)

This elaborate salad should be assembled in mounds of individual ingredients on a huge platter, not tossed. The dressing should be poured over them at the last minute. Each person selects his own portion from the platter according to his taste. Salad plates are a necessity. This salad should probably be served as a separate course.

DRESSING:
½ t. hot pepper sauce
½ t. powdered ginger
½ t. finely chopped garlic
½ c. white vinegar
 1 c. cold water

3 T. sugar
½ t. anchovy essence or
   soy sauce
1 T. salt

Combine all the ingredients in a blender and blend until smooth. Or mash the hot pepper sauce, ginger and garlic to a smooth paste in a mortar; then shake with the remaining ingredients in a jar until smooth.

SALAD:

1 c. mung bean sprouts, steamed 5 minutes and chilled
3 fresh bean curd cakes (tofu) or ¼ lb. mild white cheese, cut in ½ inch cubes

1 c. thinly shredded cabbage
1 c. thinly sliced radishes
1 c. sauerkraut, cooked
1 c. shelled peanuts, toasted

Arrange the vegetables in separate mounds on a platter. Add the dressing just before serving.

CHEESE-GARBANZO SALAD

This salad is really a cool summery main dish, since the proteins in the beans and cheese are complementary. Serves 4.

1 c. chick-pea sprouts, steamed 3 to 5 minutes and cooled
4 black olives, sliced
½ onion, minced
1 small green pepper, chopped
mayonnaise or salad dressing (if desired)

well chilled lettuce (if desired)
2 carrots, grated
1 bunch watercress, chopped
½ lb. or 1 c. grated Swiss cheese
½ c. alfalfa sprouts

Combine all ingredients. You may bind them with mayonnaise or salad dressing, and serve on a bed of lettuce.

MUNG BEAN SPROUT SANDWICH

This is a mung bean sprout sandwich as made and served by "The Corners of the Mouth," an organic food restaurant in Cambridge, Massachusetts.

SPREAD:

¼ avocado, very ripe	ripe olives may be
few sprigs watercress	substituted
¼ c. sesame or safflower	juice of 1 lemon
oil	1 clove garlic, mashed
4-6 umeboshi plums	½ c. water
(pickled, dried, salty);	

Blend these ingredients until thick and creamy. Make a "Corners of the Mouth" sandwich by sprinkling a handful of mung bean sprouts on a slice of whole wheat bread which you have spread thickly with the spread.

SALAD O'TOOLE

This is a salad devised by Chris O'Toole of Oxford. He remarks that since the carrots and cheese are identical in color, the eye is deceived and the palate is intrigued.

1 c. red Leicester cheese or orange cheddar, grated	1 c. mung bean or pea sprouts, steamed 3 minutes and cooled
1 c. raw carrot, grated to the same fineness as the cheese	½ c. mayonnaise
	2 T. chopped chives and/or parsley

Mix the ingredients together thoroughly. Chill before serving.

BERNARD JENSEN'S GREEN DELIGHT SALAD

½ T. gelatin	1 sprig mint
1 T. cold water	leaf lettuce
½ c. alfalfa sprouts	salad dressing
1 c. unsweetened pineapple juice	olives

Soften the gelatin in the water, and then melt the mixture over boiling water. Blend the sprouts, pineapple juice and mint. Then pour the gelatin mixture into the pineapple juice mixture, and combine thoroughly. Pour into a wet mold and chill until set. Turn out on a bed of leaf lettuce, and garnish with salad dressing and olives.

EGG-SALAD SUPREME

My mother, Baba Werner, invented this festive and delightful molded salad, which is a whole meal in itself.

2 8-oz. packages cream cheese
½ c. mayonnaise
2 small or 1 large packet lemon-flavored gelatin
2 c. boiling water
mustard to taste

4 c. chopped celery, onion, green pepper, sprouts, cucumber and raw cauliflower
8 to 12 hard-cooked eggs, chopped
3 T. chopped parsley
1 t. salt

Stir together the cheese, mayonnaise, gelatin and water until smooth, adding mustard to taste. Combine with the chopped vegetables, eggs, parsley and salt. Chill.

CANTONESE SALAD BOWL (China)

SALAD:
2 c. bean sprouts (steamed 2 minutes and cooled)
1 head lettuce, broken in pieces

½ c. chopped cucumber or melon, shredded
1 stalk celery, chopped
few slices red ginger pickles
10 lychees

Toss and chill. Serve with the following dressing.

SALAD DRESSING:
3 T. vegetable oil
1 T. vinegar
1 t. soy sauce

1 t. sugar
¼ t. mustard
1 clove garlic, crushed

Mix together thoroughly.

MANDARIN SALAD BOWL

2 c. sprouts, steamed
  until tender and cooled
2 T. green melon
  shredded or cucumber
2 white onions, peeled
  and sliced into rings

toasted sesame seeds
lettuce
8 pickled leeks
Chinese parsley

Toss and chill. Serve with Chinese salad dressing.

Entrees

GADO-GADO (OR PETJEL) (Java)

Surprisingly, peanut sauce is a marvelous complement to bean sprouts and vegetables. One can see why this is such a famous dish. Variations on its combinations of vegetables may be found all over Southeast Asia. It is often served with shrimp boiled in beer and drawn butter.

SAUCE:

3 T. oil
1 large onion, chopped
1 t. garlic, finely chopped
1 t. soysauce
1 c. water
1 c. peanut butter
1 coconut, coarsely grated

3 T. brown sugar
3 drops hot sauce or 1 pinch cayenne pepper
1 bay leaf
½ t. ginger
1 t. salt
4 T. lemon juice

Sauté the onion and garlic. Add the remaining ingredients and simmer 15 minutes, or until thick.

VEGETABLES:

4 small new potatoes, peeled
1 lb. scarlet runner beans
2 c. mung bean sprouts
1 bunch fresh spinach

2 hard-cooked eggs
½ small head iceberg lettuce, finely shredded
½ cucumber, unpeeled, cut into ¼ inch slices

Boil the potatoes until nearly tender. Cut into ¼ inch slices. Fry in 2 T. oil until crisp and golden. Steam beans, bean sprouts and spinach separately

until just tender; keep hot. Cut eggs crosswise
into ¼ inch slices. To serve, mound the spinach in
the center of a large platter; place around it piles
of potatoes, bean sprouts, beans (which should all
be hot), lettuce, cucumber slices and egg slices (all
cold). Pass the sauce, hot or at room temperature,
in a sauceboat.

SHRIMP EGG FOO YUNG (China)

SAUCE:

¾ c. chicken stock   1 T. cornflour dissolved
 1 T. soy sauce   in 2 T. stock or water
½ t. salt

Heat the chicken stock and add the soy sauce
and salt. Add the cornflour mixture, and stir until
thickened. Remove from heat, but keep warm.

PANCAKES:

1 c. mung bean sprouts   6 T. oil
3 or 4 mushrooms, diced   3 eggs
½ lb. raw shrimp,   rice (if desired)
  shelled, cleaned, diced peas (if desired)
  small

Stir-fry shrimp until pink. Beat eggs, add
shrimp, sprouts and mushrooms. Fry each of 6
pancakes in 1 T. oil. Serve with rice and peas.
(Peas are not traditional.) Serve the sauce separately. Roast pork may be substituted for the
shrimp.

SQUID WITH BEAN SPROUTS (China)

1 lb. fresh squid	1 T. cornflour
2 T. oil	1 T. sherry
1 clove garlic, crushed	1 t. sugar
1 inch green ginger, crushed	½ t. salt
	3 T. stock
2 c. bean sprouts, blanched	1 T. thin oyster sauce

Wash and clean squid thoroughly, removing the thin membrane. Slash crosswise and lengthwise, making a diamond pattern; cut diagonally in pieces about ½ inch long. Heat pan, add oil, garlic and ginger, and sauté squid until it curls. Blanch bean sprouts and add. Mix. Add and mix in cornflour, sherry, sugar, salt, stock and oyster sauce. Cook 1 minute more.

EGG ROLLS WITH SHRIMP AND PORK

FILLING:

½ lb. lean pork, finely ground	1 T. cornstarch in 2 T. water
½ lb. raw shrimp, shelled and diced	½ t. sugar
1 T. Chinese rice wine or dry sherry	2 to 3 mushrooms, chopped
1 T. soy sauce	4 stalks celery, chopped
	2 t. salt
	2 c. bean sprouts

Stir-fry pork in 1 T. oil for 2 minutes. Add shrimp, wine, soy sauce, cornstarch, sugar and mushrooms. Continue cooking 1 minute, and set aside. Stir-fry celery 5 minutes. Add salt and bean sprouts (well-drained), and meat.

WRAPPERS:

2 c. flour	3/4 c. cold water
1/2 t. salt	1 egg, beaten

Mix into a stiff dough, knead 5 minutes, rest 30 minutes and roll out thin. Cut into 16 7-inch squares. Spread each square with filling, leaving room to fold in sides, and roll into cylinders.

FRYING:
2 c. peanut oil or light oil

Heat oil to 375° F. and deep-fry the rolls a few at a time for 3 to four minutes.

CHICKEN WITH BEAN SPROUTS (China)

1 chicken (2-3 lbs.)	2 c. bean sprouts
salt	1 T. sugar
2 T. soy sauce	1 c. chicken stock
2 T. oil	1 T. cornstarch
1 clové garlic	1 T. mushroom sauce
1 inch fresh green ginger, crushed	

Cut chicken into small bits and season with salt and soy sauce. Heat the oil and stir-fry the seasoned chicken with garlic and ginger until it changes color. Remove from pan but keep hot. Then stir-fry bean sprouts with the sugar for 1 minute and add the chicken stock and cornstarch mixed with mushroom sauce. Cook 1 minute. Add seasoned chicken and reheat. Serve with fried rice. Cooked chicken may be used; in that case, omit first cooking.

LOBSTER FRIED RICE (China)

1 c. rice, cooked and chilled	1 t. sugar
	3 eggs
1 c. bean sprouts	salt
oil	1 c. cooked lobster meat
1 inch green ginger, shredded	3 shallots, chopped
	1 T. soy sauce

Stir-fry the bean sprouts with the oil, ginger and sugar. Make a thin omelet with the eggs and salt and cut into strips.

Stir-fry the rice with oil. Add the lobster, sprouts and shallots, and mix well. Add the soy sauce, and serve very hot with egg strips on top.

VEGETABLE-MEAT PANCAKES (Korea)
(Ku Chul Paan)

This is a real assembly job. The result is a fascinating and beautiful dish.

¼ lb. beef, finely chopped	3 eggs
1 T. green onion	1 cucumber
¾ t. chopped garlic	15 fresh mushrooms
4 t. toasted sesame seed	1 carrot
1 t. sugar	1 bunch spinach, steamed
2 T. oil	
10 t. soy sauce	1 c. bean sprouts
¾ t. salt	1 c. flour
	1 c. water

FILLING:

Prepare 8 separate portions of filling, as follows (you may use the same pan each time):

1. Stir-fry the beef, after adding to it 1 t. chopped green onion, ¼ t. chopped garlic, ½ t. sesame seed, ½ t. sugar, ½ t. oil, 1 T. soy sauce and ½ t. salt.

2 and 3. Separate the egg whites and yolks. Beat. Fry separately in thin layers; shred into fine strips, 2 inches long.

4. Cut the cucumber into thin circles and pat dry. Stir-fry 2 minutes in 1 t. oil with ½ t. onion, ⅛ t. garlic and 1½ t. sesame seed.

5. Cut the mushrooms into fine strips. Mix together ½ t. sesame seed, ½ t. sugar, 1 t. oil and 1 t. soy sauce. Add this mixture to the mushrooms and stir-fry for 2 minutes.

6. Cut the carrot into fine strips 2 inches long. Boil 2 minutes and drain. Add ½ t. onion. ⅛ t. garlic, ½ t. sesame seed, ¼ t. oil and 2 t. soy sauce.

7. Steam the bean sprouts until tender. Add ½ t. onion, ⅛ t. garlic, ½ t. sesame seed, ¼ t. oil and 2 t. soy sauce.

8. Season the steamed spinach with ½ t. onion, ⅛ t. garlic, ½ t. sesame seed, ¼ t. oil and 2 t. soy sauce.

PANCAKES:

Mix flour and water with ¼ t. salt until smooth. Fry in a hot oiled skillet 8 paper-thin circles 4 inches across.

Arrange the cakes in the center of a platter, and the 8 foods around the cakes. Put a very small portion of each food on each cake and roll it up. Serve hot.

CHOW MEIN (China)

Although chop suey is unheard of in China and was probably invented in the U. S., chow mein is an ancient Chinese snack or light meal. It can be made with beef, pork, shrimp or chicken. The last three meats are probably more authentic, for beef was rarely used in China until recently. Serves 4.

½ lb. pork, beef, shrimp or chicken, cut in fine strips
1 T. oil
2 large onions, sliced
2 stalks celery, chopped
1 small can bamboo shoots, drained

¼ lb. mushrooms, sliced
2 c. bean sprouts
2 T. cornstarch
½ c. soup stock
½ T. powdered ginger
1 t. sugar
3 T. soy sauce

Stir-fry the meat in ½ T. oil until cooked (2 minutes); remove from pan. Add the onions, celery, bamboo shoots, mushrooms and sprouts to the pan and stir-fry 1 minute. Mix together the cornstarch, stock, ginger, sugar and soy sauce. Add to the vegetables and boil 1 minute. Add the meat, mix well, and heat through. Serve with boiled rice.

SUKIYAKI (Japan)

I am not sure whether sprouts are entirely traditional in this famous dish, but they are a delightful addition. The most elaborate way to cook sukiyaki is in an electric skillet at the table, with the guests assembled. Have all the vegetables and the meat prepared, add them in the order given. The whole ritual should occupy about 10 minutes. Serves 4.

1 to 2 lbs, very thinly sliced beef

3 T. cooking oil

1 medium onion, thinly sliced

½ lb. soybean curd (tofu) in ¾ inch cubes (optional)

6 scallions cut into 1 inch pieces

6 stalks celery or chinese cabbage, chopped

½ lb. mushrooms, thinly sliced

1 lb. watercress or spinach, shredded

1 c. mung bean sprouts

½ c. soy sauce

1 c. stock

1 t. sugar

boiled rice for 4

1 raw egg

Stir-fry the beef in the oil about 3 minutes. Then push aside and stir-fry the vegetables, one at a time, beginning with those that need longer cooking (as indicated by the order in which they are listed above.) Have a cup with the soy sauce and stock in it near the pan; add a few spoonfuls of this liquid mixture occasionally to keep the vegetables moist. Sprinkle the sugar over the vegetables while stirring them. The vegetables should not become soft, but remain crisp and brightly colored—just barely cooked before they are combined with the beef. Serve over boiled rice and pass additional soy sauce. As a truly authentic touch, beat the raw egg in a small bowl and pass it as a dip for pieces of the sukiyaki.

BAKED STUFFED PEPPERS

1 onion, chopped
1 T. oil
½ lb. raw lean ground
 beef
2 c. rye sprouts
1 t. salt

pinch each of pepper,
 basil, savory and
 marjoram
4 large red or green bell
 peppers, steamed 10
 minutes
1 small can tomato
 sauce

Sauté onion in 1 T. oil. Mix in beef, and stir until it loses its red color. Mix in rye sprouts and flavorings, and stuff into peppers. Cover with tomato sauce. Bake at 350° F. for 20 minutes. Two cups of cooked rice may be substituted for the beef. Serves 4.

ADUKI HASH

1 c. aduki bean sprouts
½ c. water or broth
1 onion, chopped
¼ t. pepper
pinch of marjoram
1 T. salt
2 T. butter

1 clove garlic, finely
 minced
1 c. leftover cooked beef
 or tongue, diced
1 green or red bell
 pepper, diced

Simmer sprouts in water or broth until tender (about 10 to 12 minutes). Add other ingredients and heat only until the meat is heated through. Do not boil. Serves 2 to 3.

SAVORY MEAT LOAF

An unusually flavorful meat loaf.

2 slices bread	1½ t. salt
½ c. milk	¼ t. basil
1 egg	2 T. chopped parsley
2 onions, shredded	¼ t. pepper
1 c. chick-pea sprouts	sprinkle of paprika
1 garlic clove, minced	2 strips bacon
1 lb. lean minced beef	1 small can tomato
or beef/pork/veal	sauce (optional)

Soak the bread in the milk and egg, beaten together. Add the onions, sprouts, garlic, meat, salt, basil, parsley and pepper. Mix well, and mold into loaf. Sprinkle with paprika. Place 2 strips of bacon on top. Bake at 350° F. for 1 hour. Tomato sauce may be poured over loaf before baking.

KATE'S THREE-SPROUT CURRY (vegetarian)

2 medium onions, sliced	2 T. oil
2 large carrots, grated	2 T. flour
2 stalks celery, chopped	1 T. curry powder
3 T. oil	2 c. milk
1 c. fenugreek sprouts	1 t. salt
1 c. alfalfa sprouts	1 t. nutmeg
1 c. mung bean sprouts	½ c. peanut butter

Sauté onions, carrots and celery in 3 T. oil until soft and golden. To make the sauce, combine 2 T. oil, flour, and curry powder; and, placing on medium heat, add the milk slowly, stirring all the time until the mixture thickens. Add salt, nutmeg and peanut butter. Stir well. Combine with the sautéed vegetables and the sprouts. Cook just 3 minutes more, or until the sprouts are hot through. Serve over brown rice, buckwheat groats or steamed whole wheat.

SOYBEAN SALAMAGUNDI (vegetarian)

The name of this ratatouille is an American term for
a vegetable melee.

3 T. olive oil
3 onions, sliced
1 clove garlic, minced
5 small zucchini,
  unpeeled and diced
2 or 3 green peppers,
  diced
1 medium eggplant,
  unpeeled and diced

1 can tomatoes or 3
  small tomatoes, peeled
  and chopped
1 c. soybean sprouts
1 T. salt
½ t. pepper
pinch of basil

Sauté onions and garlic in oil until tender. Add
everything else. Simmer 15 minutes or until the
vegetables are blended and tender.

BEAN SPROUT AND CHICKEN SOUFFLÉ

This dish was served at Governor Dewey's luncheon
and pictured in the July 19, 1943 issue of *Life*. Serves
4.

3 T. butter
3 T. flour
1 c. milk
1 t. salt

4 eggs
1 c. chicken meat, cubed
1 c. blanched soy sprouts,
  steamed 20 minutes
  and chopped coarsely

Make a white sauce by blending the butter and
flour and stirring in the milk gradually over a low
heat. Add the salt. Separate the eggs; beat the
yolks and mix into the white sauce. Then fold in the
chicken and sprouts. Beat the egg whites until
stiff, fold in, and gently push the mixture into a
well-greased 2 qt. soufflé dish. Set the soufflé dish
into a pan of hot water 1 inch deep. Bake in a slow
oven, 300-325° F., 40 to 50 minutes. Serve immediately with a mild cheese sauce.

SAVORY SOYBEAN SPROUTS

This recipe resembles the recipe for Boston baked beans. It does not require the hours of cooking, however, that the other recipe calls for.

2 c. soybean sprouts	1 onion, chopped
1 c. stock or consommé	½ c. tomato purée
½ t. black pepper	1 T. Worcestershire
2 t. salt	sauce
2 T. butter	3 T. brown sugar
1 clove garlic, minced	4 T. chopped parsley

Drop sprouts into boiling stock. Simmer 10 minutes, or until tender. Add the remaining ingredients, uncover, and continue to simmer to evaporate the liquid to a thick sauce. Add 4 T. chopped parsley. Serve hot or cold.

ALMOND-MUSHROOM CHOP SUEY

Although chop suey was probably invented by Americans, or at least in the U. S. by a Chinese cook, the method used in making it can be authentic, and it can be a very nice light dish.

2 large onions, chopped	2 T. soy sauce
2 stalks celery, chopped	1 T. cornstarch
1 T. oil	(optional)
1 green bell pepper, sliced	bed of cooked brown rice
1 c. mung bean sprouts	¾ c. toasted almonds, chopped
½ lb. fresh mushrooms, sliced	

Stir-fry onions and celery in 1 T. oil for 1 minute. Add green pepper, sprouts and mushrooms. Stir well, cover and let heat thoroughly. Add soy sauce. (If a thick sauce is desired, add 1 T. cornstarch to the soy sauce.) Serve on a mound of brown or converted rice. Sprinkle generously with almonds.

Vegetable Dishes

These are dishes smaller than the entrees because they are meant to act as accompaniments to main dishes. They can be served to add interest to a rather plain meat course. Or, made in a larger quantity, many of them can be served as main dishes.

RYE SPROUT PILAF

4 T. butter	½ lb. mushrooms, sliced
1 c. sprouted rye or	2 T. chopped parsley
wheat, drained well	1 t. salt
½ c. water or consommé	

Melt butter in a heavy pan, and sauté sprouts and mushrooms 5 minutes. Add water or consommé and simmer until evaporated. Season with salt and garnish with parsley.

BEAN SPROUTS WITH SAVOURY SAUCE (Korea)
(Khong Na-Mool)

A side dish commonly served.

2 c. bean sprouts	1½ t. oil
2½ T. soy sauce	1 t. salt
2 t. toasted sesame	red pepper
seeds	2 green onions

Steam sprouts until tender. Add everything except the onion tops. Cut these into ½ inch lengths and add at the last.

RICE AND BEAN SPROUTS (Korea)
(Kong Na-Mool Pahb)

Rice is very commonly served in Korea, sometimes with the addition of bean sprouts.

1 c. raw rice	1 clove garlic, chopped
2 c. cold water	2 t. toasted sesame seed
1 c. soybean sprouts	2 T. soy sauce
1 green onion	1 t. oil

Combine all ingredients, bring to a boil, reduce heat to very low and steam 30 minutes. Do not stir or remove lid while cooking.

LENTIL SPROUTS LEBANESE

1 large onion, sliced	2 T. whole green lentils,
2 stalks celery, sliced	sprouted
2 T. olive oil	1/4 t. powdered basil
1 can of tomatoes or 3 small tomatoes	

Sauté onions and celery until soft but not brown. Add other ingredients and simmer, uncovered, 5 to 8 minutes.

SPROUTS WITH CELERY

2 T. oil	2 T. soy sauce
1 stalk celery, chopped	1 t. salt
1 large onion, chopped	1/4 t. pepper
1 c. green soybean sprouts	

Sauté all the vegetables together. Add salt, pepper and soy sauce. Cook 5 minutes, or until tender.

CREAMED SPROUTS EN CASSEROLE

2 c. cooked soybean
  sprouts
1 can whole-kernel corn
2 c. white sauce (or
  richer bechamel sauce)

4 T. minced green pepper
4 T. parsley
seasoning to taste
melba toast crumbs or
  wheat germ

Mix all the ingredients together except the crumbs, pour into a baking dish, sprinkle crumbs or wheat germ on top and bake for 25 minutes at 350° F.

Breads and Stuffings

ZUNI WHEAT SPROUT BREAD (Arizona, U. S. A.)
(He Palokia)

2 c. wheat sprouts	5 c. whole wheat flour
4 T. warm water	1 T. salt
1 T. sugar or honey	2 c. warm water
1 T. (or 1 cake) yeast	3 T. oil or melted butter
½ c. non-instant	3 T. honey or molasses
powdered milk	
(optional)	

Sprout wheat just until root is as long as grain (3 days in a warm room). Combine 4 T. warm water, sugar, and yeast and let stand until foamy (about 10 minutes). If desired, mix ½ c. powdered milk with the flour and salt before adding yeast mixture. Combine water, oil and honey with the wheat sprouts and stir this mixture into the flour. Beat or stir until the batter is smooth, shiny and elastic (about 1 minute). This traditional way to bake this bread is between 2 hot flat rocks. A similar result is obtained by dropping about a cupful of batter onto a greased cookie sheet; it spreads out into a flat round, about 1 inch thick. Bake at 350° F. for about 30 minutes. If baked in a loaf pan, wheat sprout bread resembles a nutbread.

SPROUTED WHEAT PANCAKES

1 c. flour	2 T. oil
1 t. salt	1 c. milk
1 T. sugar	2 eggs
2 t. baking powder	1 c. wheat sprouts

Combine the dry ingredients. Then combine the liquids, add to the dry ingredients and mix well. After pouring each pancake into a hot, greased skillet to bake, sprinkle on it 1 T. sprouts. Don't combine the wheat sprouts with the batter, as they will sink to the bottom, and all the sprouts will be in the last pancakes.

WHEAT SPROUT STUFFING

I've never seen a recipe for anything like this. The sprouts are slightly chewy in the bread dressing, and the taste is delicious!

1 small onion, chopped	2 T. melted butter
2 stalks celery, chopped	1 t. salt
1 c. wheat sprouts	½ t. pepper
1 c. whole wheat bread crumbs	sage or thyme, if desired

Chop onion and celery till fine. Toss with sprouts and crumbs. Pour melted butter over all and toss again. Add salt and pepper, and sage or thyme if desired. Will stuff a 3 to 4 lb. fowl.

ALFALFA SPROUT BREAD

1 small potato	1 pkg. yeast (½ oz.)
water or milk	2 c. alfalfa sprouts
5 T. honey	4 c. whole wheat flour or
2 t. salt	unbleached white flour
2 T. oil	

Cut potato in small pieces. Cook till very soft in water to cover. Cool to lukewarm. Mash or liquify potato; add enough water or milk to make 1½ c. liquid. Add honey, salt and oil to liquid, and crumble yeast in. Let stand 10 minutes, or until the yeast begins to bubble and foam. Add 2 cups of the flour, and the alfalfa sprouts. Mix. Then add enough flour to make a stiff dough. Knead well. Allow to rise once, 30 to 60 minutes, punch down, and allow to rise again. Make into loaves or buns, and allow to rise a third time. Bake at 350° F. for 1 hour.

Desserts

SPROUTED WHEAT BALLS

1 c. wheat sprouts
1 c. cream cheese

1 c. ground nuts
1 c. raisins

Blend together the sprouts, cheese, nuts and raisins. Shape into balls as large as walnuts. Roll in grated toasted coconut or toasted wheat germ. Keep refrigerated.

BERNARD JENSEN'S CHEWS

1 c. sprouted wheat or
   barley
1 c. almonds or cashews

1 c. seeded raisins
pinch salt
grated coconut

Combine the sprouts, nuts and raisins, and add a pinch of salt. Grind in a meat grinder. Shape into balls the size of a walnut and roll in grated coconut.

PANOCHA

This recipe calls for flour made from sun-dried wheat sprouts rather than fresh whole sprouts. Use a flour grinder or coffee mill to make this flour. This recipe is from New Mexico (U. S. A.) Extension Circular 250.

5 c. sprouted wheat
   flour
2½ c. whole wheat flour

9 c. boiling water
2 c. sugar (if desired)
4 T. butter

Mix the sprouted wheat flour and whole wheat flour thoroughly. Add half of the boiling water, and stir well. Set aside and cover. Let stand for 15 minutes; then add the rest of the water. (If sugar is used, caramelize the sugar, add a cup of boiling water, and, when the sugar is dissolved, add to the flour mixture.) Boil the mixture for 2 hours, add butter, and place uncovered in the oven for 1 hour or until it is quite thick and deep brown. Some people prefer to leave sugar out, as the sprouted wheat has its own sugar.

UNBAKED FRUITCAKE

This makes a lovely Christmas cake.

½ lb. pitted dates	½ lb. dried currants
½ lb. chopped figs	½ lb. dried apricots
½ lb. seedless raisins	½ lb. wheat sprouts
½ lb. seeded raisins	4 T. honey
½ lb. shelled almonds	8 oz. creamed coconut
½ lb. dried bananas	

Put the dates, figs, raisins, almonds, bananas, currants, apricots and wheat sprouts through a coarse meat grinder. Add honey and mix well. Press firmly into a loaf pan. Melt creamed coconut and spread over the top. Chill 24 hours. Slice very thin. Keep cool.

CHRISTMAS CAKE

Sprouted wheat in this cake makes it seem very full of nuts. If you add ¼ cup of chopped almonds and ¾ cup of sprouts, no one will realize that all the crunch is not almonds.

1 c. butter	½ t. ground cloves
1 c. brown sugar	¼ c. ground almonds
4 eggs, beaten	½ c. raisins, chopped
1 c. flour	½ c. fruit peel, chopped
1 t. salt	½ c. glacé cherries
1 t. ground ginger	½ c. almonds, chopped
½ t. mixed spice	¾ c. sprouted wheat
½ t. ground cinnamon	½ wineglass brandy

Cream together the butter and sugar. Add the beaten eggs and mix well. Combine the flour with the spices and sift. Then dust the chopped fruits, almonds and sprouts with ¼ c. of this flour mixture. Combine the butter and flour mixtures with the dusted ingredients. Add the brandy and mix well. Pack into an 8 inch tube pan or a 9 x 5 inch loaf pan lined with greased paper. Bake in a moderate oven 350° F. for 1 hour. Reduce the heat to 300° F. and bake 2 more hours.

REFERENCES

1. Abrahamsen, M. 1965. Some aspects of the carbohydrate metabolism of germinating soybean [*Glycine max*] seedlings in relation to levels of carbohydrates and carbohydrate precursors. *Diss. Absts.* 25: 4368-4369.

2. Adkins, D. M. 1920. Digestibility of germinated beans. *Biochem. Jour.* 14: 637-641.

3. Allison, R. S. 1943. *Sea Diseases.* London: John Bale Med. Publ., Ltd.

4. Altschul, A. M. 1965. *Proteins: Their Chemistry and Politics.* New York: Basic Books, Inc.

5. Anonymous. 1943. Plant beans Monday, eat 'em Thursday: Chinese mung bean sprouts. *Popular Mechanics* 79: 78-79.

6. Anonymous. 1943. Meat substitute: sprouted soy beans are high in protein, fat, minerals and vitamins. *Science Newsletter* 43: 326.

7. Anonymous. 1943. Governor Dewey sponsors them as partial solution to food crisis. *Life* 15: 45.

8. Anonymous. 1943. Soybeans of recent crop needed for making sprouts. *Science Newsletter* 44: 264.

9. Anonymous. 1943. Victory garden in a flowerpot. *Popular Science* 143: 177-178.

10. Anonymous. 1943. How to sprout soybeans. *Ladies Home Journal.* 60: 63.

11. Banerjee, S., and Banerjee, R. 1950. Studies on the biosynthesis of nicotinic acid. I. Biosynthesis of nicotinic acid by germinating pulses. *Ind. Jour. Med. Res.* 38: 153-160.

12. Banerjee, S.; Ghosh, N. C., and Nandi, N. 1951. Effect of germination on the nicotinic acid, nicotinuric acid, N'-methylnicotinamide, and trigonel-

line values of pulses and cereals. *Ind. Jour. Med. Res.* 39: 447-452.

13. Banerjee, S.; Rohatgi, K. S.; Banerjee, M.; Chattopadhyay, D. P.; and Chattopadhyay, H. P. 1955. Pyroxidine, inositol, and vitamin K contents of germinated pulses. *Food Res.* 20: 545.

14. Banerjee, S.; Guha Roy, A. R.; and Ghosh, P. K. 1959. Folic acid metabolism in germinating seeds. *Food Res.* 24: 332-334.

15. Beaglehole, J. C., ed. 1963. ENDEAVOUR *Journal of Joseph Banks.* Sydney.

16. Beeskow, H. C. 1943. Bean sprouts: their preparation and properties. *Tech. Bull.* 184, Michigan State Coll. Agric. Exper. Sta.

17. Bhagvat, K., and Narasinga Ras, K. K. P. 1942. Vitamin C in germinating grains. *Ind. Jour. Med. Res.* 30: 493-504.
    Bircher-Benner, R. *See* no. 140.

18. Bois, D. 1914. Germes de Soja et Germes de Haricot Mungo, un produit alimentaire faussement denomme. *Bull. de la Société Nationale d'Acclimatation de France.*

19. Boulter, D., and Barber, J. T. 1963. Amino-acid metabolism in germinating seeds of *Vicia faba* L. in relation to their biology. *New Phytol.* 62: 301-316.

20. Bretschneider, E. 1892. *Botanicon Sinicum,* vols. I, II. Shanghai.

21. Bretschneider, E. 1895-1896. *Botanicon Sinicum.* vol. III. (Materia Medica of Chinese). *Jour. Royal Asiatic Soc.,* Great Britain and Ireland, North China Branch 29: 623 pp.

22. Brown, B. E.; Meade, E. M.; and Butterfield, J. R. 1962. The effect of germination upon the fat of the soybean. *Jour. Amer. Oil Chem. Soc.* 39: 327-330.

23. Burkholder, P. R. 1943. Vitamins in dehydrated seeds and sprouts. *Science* 97: 562-564.

24. Burkholder, P. R., and McVeigh, I. 1942. The increase of B vitamins in germinating seeds. *Proc. Nat. Acad. Sci.* 28: 440-446.

25. Burkholder, P. R., and McVeigh, I. 1945. Vita-

min content of some mature and germinated legume seeds. *Plant Physiol.* 20: 301-306.

26. Butt, J. M.; Hamid, A.; and Shah, F. H. 1965. Changes in vitamin "C" contents of germinating seeds, Black Bengal grams (*Cicer arietinum*). *Pakistan J. Sci. Res.* 17: 164-168.

27. Carpenter, T. M., and Steggerda, M. 1939. The food of the present-day Navajo Indians of New Mexico and Arizona. *Jour. Nutrition* 18: 297-305.

28. Catsimpoolas, N.; Campbell, T. G.; and Meyer, E. W. 1968. Immunochemical study of changes in reserve proteins of germinating soybean seeds. *Plant Physiol.* 43: 799-805.

29. Chattopadhyay, H. P., and Banerjee, S. 1951. Effect of germination on the carotene content of pulses and cereals. *Science* 113: 600.

30. Chattopadhyay, H. P., and Banerjee, S. 1951. Studies on the choline content of some common Indian pulses and cereals both before and during the course of germination. *Food Res.* 16: 230-232.

31. Chattopadhyay, H. P., and Banerjee, S. 1952. Effect of germination on the total tocopherol content of pulses and cereals. *Food Res.* 17: 402-403.

32. Chattopadhyay, H. P., and Banerjee, S. 1953. Effect of germination on biological values of proteins and the trypsin-inhibitor activity of common Indian pulses. *Ind. Jour. Med. Res.* 41: 185-189.

33. Cheldelin, V. H., and Lane, R. L. 1943. B vitamins in germinating seeds. *Proc. Soc. Exper. Biol. and Med.* 54: 53-55.

34. Chen, P. S. 1973. *Soybeans for Health and a Longer Life.* New Canaan: Keats Publishing, Inc. 85.

35. Cheng, Y. Y. S. 1944. The effect of sprouting on the nutritive value of soybeans: the ascorbic acid content and the protein quality. Unpubl. Ph. D. thesis, Cornell University.

36. Chick, H., and Delf, E. M. 1919. The anti-scorbutic value of dry and germinated seeds. *Biochem. Jour.* 13: 199-218.

37. Cocking, E. C., and Yemm, E. W. 1961. Synthesis of amino acids and proteins in barley seedlings. *New Phytol.* 60: 103-116.

38. Cook, J. 1777. *A Voyage Toward the South Pole and Round the World*. London: W. and A. Strahan.

39. Davis, A. 1954. *Let's Eat Right to Keep Fit*. New York: Harcourt Brace Jovanovich, Inc.

40. Davis, A. 1965. *Let's Get Well*. New York: Harcourt Brace Jovanovich, Inc.

41. Davis, A. 1959. *Let's Have Healthy Children*. New York: Harcourt Brace Jovanovich, Inc.

42. De, H. N., and Barai, S. C. 1949. Study of the mechanism of biosynthesis of ascorbutic acid during germination. *Ind. Jour. Med. Res.* 37: 101-111.

43. Delf, M. 1922. Studies in experimental scurvy with special reference to the antiscorbutic properties of some South African foodstuffs. *Lancet* (London) 1: 576-579.

44. Desikachar, H. S. R., and De, S. S. 1947. Role of inhibitors in soybean. *Science* 106: 421-422.

45. Dodds, M. L. 1959. Vitamin C In Food. *The Yearbook of Argiculture*, 1959. U. S. D. A. 150-161.

46. Drennan, D. S. H. 1962. Physiological studies of germination in the genus *Avena*. II. Changes in some metabolites during the germination of grains of *A. sativa*. *New Phytol.* 61: 261-265.

47. Dunn, M. S.; Camien, M. N.; Shankman, S.; and Block, H. 1948. Amino acids in lupine and soybean seeds and sprouts. *Arch. Biochem.* 18: 195-200.

48. Embrey, H. and Wang, T. C. 1921. Analyses of some Chinese foods. *China Med. Jour.* 35: 247-257.

49. Erkama, J., and Pettersson, N. 1950. Vitamin K in germinating peas. *Acta Chem. Scand* 4: 922-925.

50. Evans, R. J., and Bandemer, S. L. 1967. Nutritive value of legume seed proteins. *Jour. Agric. Food Chem.* 15: 439-445.

51. Everson, G. J.; Steenbock, H.; Cederquist, D. C.;

and Parsons, H. T. 1944. The effect of germination, the stage of maturity, and the variety upon the nutritive value of the soybean protein. *Jour. Nutr.* 27: 225-229.

52. Fohn-Hansen, L. 1944. How to sprout soybeans and other seeds for table use. *Alaska Univ. Agric. Exper. Leaflet* 142.

53. Folkes, B. F., and Yemm, E. W. 1958. The respiration of barley plants. X. Respiration and the metabolism of amino acids and proteins in germinating grain. *New Phytol.* 57: 106-131.

54. French, C. E.; Berryman, G. H.; Goorley, J. T.; Harper, H. A.; Harkness, D. M.; and Thacker, E. J. 1944. The production of vitamins in germinated peas, soybeans, and other beans. *Jour. Nutrition* 28: 63-70.

55. Gallup, W. D., and Reder, R. E. 1944. Sprouted cowpeas as a source of protein and vitamins. *Proc. Oklahoma Acad. Sci.* 24: 53-55.

56. Gerstenberger, H. J. 1921. Malt soup extract as an antiscorbutic. *Amer. Jour. Dis. Child.* 21: 315-326.

57. Gibbins, L. N., and Norris, F. W. 1963. Vitamins in germination. Distribution of inositol during the germination of the dwarf bean, *Phaseolus vulgaris. Biochem. Jour.* 86: 64-67.

58. Gilbert, S. G., and Sell, H. M. 1957. Biochemical changes during germination of the tung seed. *Plant Physiol.* 32: 668-674.

59. Grieg, E. 1917. The sprouting capacity of grains issued as rations to troops. *Ind. Jour. Med. Res.* 4: 818-823.

60. Hall, G. S., and Laidman, D. L. 1968. The pattern and control of isoprenoid quinone and tocopherol metabolism in the germinating grain of wheat. *Biochem. Jour.* 108: 475-482.

61. Haugen, G., and Pijoan, M. 1946. Certain factors affecting vitamin C content of bean sprouts. *Arch. Biochem.* 10: 227-234.

62. Harris, L. J., and Ray, S. N. 1933. Specificity of hexuronic acid as anti-scorbutic factor. *Biochem. Jour.* 27: 580.

63. Hermano, H. J., and Sepulveda, G. 1934. The vi-

tamin contents of Philippine foods, III. Vitamin B in various fruits and vegetables. *Philip. Jour. Sci.* 54: 61-73.

64. Hess, A. F. 1920. *Scurvy, Past and Present.* Philadelphia: J. B. Lippincott.
Hiatt, D. R., *See* no. 141.

65. Hodges, L. M. 1943. Are you neglecting the wonder bean? Reader's Digest 43: 107-109. [Condensed from National Miller and American Miller.]

66. Hooker, J. D. 1896. Journal of Sir Joseph Banks during Captain Cook's first voyage. London.

67. Hopkins, R. H., and Krause, C. B. 1940. *Biochemistry Applied to Malting and Brewing.* New York: D. van Nostrand Company.

68. Howarth, A. A. 1925. The soybean as human food. Chinese Govt. Bureau of Economic Information. Peking.

69. Huber, R. E., and Zalik, S. 1963. Lipid and protein in germinating and developing flaxseed *Linum usitatissimum* L. *Canad. Jour. Biochem. Physiol.* 41: 745-754.
Hunter, B. T. *See* no. 142.

70. Hymowitz, T. 1970. On the domestication of the soybean. *Econ. Bot.* 24: 408-421.

71. Iengar, N. G. C.; Jayaraman, V.; and Rau, Y. V. S. 1955. Thiamine contents of some Indian foodstuffs during germination. *Ann. Biochem. and Exptl. Med.* 15: 49-54.

72. Jaeger, E. 1943. First aid to diets. *Nature Magazine* 36: 190.
Jensen, B. *See* no. 143.
Jones, D. van G. *See* no. 144.

73. Kakade, M. L., and Evans, R. J. 1966. Effect of soaking and germinating on the nutritive value of navy beans. *Jour. Food. Sci.* 31: 781-783.

74. Kale, F. S. 1937. *Soya Bean: Its Value in Dietetics, Cultivation, and Uses with 300 Recipes.* Shanker Tekri, Baroda, India: F. Doctor & Co.

75. Kuppuswamy, S.; Meena. Rao, J.; Srinivasan, M.; and Subranmanyan, M. 1958. Ascorbic acid in germinating seeds of *Sesbania grandiflora* Pers. *Current Sci.* 27: 343-345.

76. Kasugai, A. 1964. Studies on the relation between germination and alpha amylase formation in mung bean sprout *Phaseolus aureus* Roxb. *Agric. Biol. Chem.* 28: A4.

77. Khan, M. M. 1942. Scurvy in the famine areas of Hissar District, Punjab. *Ind. Med. Gaz.* 77: 6.

78. Kuhn, W. F. 1947. Improving and modernizing the growing of Chinese bean sprouts. *Canning Trade* 70: 7.

79. Lager, M. 1945. *The Useful Soybean.* New York: McGraw-Hill.

80. Langley, R. A. 1942. Mung beans. *Better Homes and Gardens* 20: 8-9.

81. Larson, B. 1963. Der Starkeabbau im Pansen bei Futterung gekeimten Getreides. II. Futterungsversuche mit Malz und mit gekeimten Getreide. *Zeit. Tierphysiol, Tierernachrung, u. Futtermittelkunde* 18: 209-215. [Seen in abstract only.]

82. Lee, F. A., and Whitcombe, J. 1945. Effect of freezing, preservation and cooking on vitamin content of green soybeans and soybean sprouts. *Amer. Dietet. Assoc. Jour.* 21: 696-697.

83. Lee, S. L. 1966. *Korean Folk Medicine.* Monograph Series #3. South Korea: Seoul Nat. Univ.

84. Lee, W.-Y., and Read, B. E. 1936. The effect of light on the production and distribution of ascorbic acid in germinated soybeans. *Jour. Chinese Chem. Soc.* 4: 208-218.

85. Liener, I. E., ed. 1969. *Toxic Constituents of Plant Foodstuffs.* New York: Academic Press.

86. Lounsbury, T. F. 1943. Kitchen-garden with soybeans. *Better Homes and Gardens* 21: 20-21.

87. Lugg, J. W. H., and Weller, R. A. 1943. Germinating seeds as a source of vitamin C in human nutrition. *Australian Jour. Exper. Biol. and Med. Sci.* 21: 111-114.

88. MacBride, D. 1768. Historical Account of the New Method of Treating the Scurvy at Sea.

89. Marcus, A., and Feeley, J. 1964. Activation of protein synthesis in the imbibation phase of seed germination. *Proc. Nat. Acad. Sci. U. S. A.* 51: 1075-1079.

90. Mattingly, J. P., and Bird, H. R. 1945. Effect of heating under various conditions, and of sprouting on the nutritive value of soybean oil meals and soybeans. *Poultry Sci.* 24: 344-352.

Mayer, A. and Poljakoff-Maber A. *See* no. 145.

91. McKinney, L. L.; Weakley, F. B.; Campbell, R. E.; and Cowan, J. C. 1958. Changes in the composition of soybeans on sprouting. *Jour. Amer. Oil Chem. Soc.* 35: 364-366.

92. Merrill, E. D. 1954. The botany of Cook's voyages. *Chronica Botanica* 14 (5, 6).

93. Miller, C. D., and Hair, D. B. 1928. The vitamin content of mung bean sprouts. *Jour. Home Econ.* 20: 263-271.

94. Mukherji, S.; Dey, B.; and Sircar, S. M. 1968. Changes in nicotinic acid content and its nucleotide derivatives of rice and wheat seeds during germination. *Physiol. Plant.* 21: 360-368.

95. Nada, I. A. A., and Rafaat, A. 1955. Carbohydrate changes during germination of *Vicia faba* seeds. *Ind. Jour. Agric. Sci.* 25: 271-280.

96. Naik, M. S., and Narayana, N. 1960. Biosynthesis of riboflavin in Bengal gram seedlings. *Ann. Biochem. and Exptl. Med.* 20: 237-242.

97. Naik, M. S., and Narayana, N., 1963. Production of riboflavin in Bengal gram plants and the effect of light on riboflavin in the seedlings. *Ann. Biochem. and Exptl. Med.* 23: 385-390.

98. Nandi, D. L. 1958. Studies on the changes in free amino acids and B-vitamin content of some leguminous seeds during germination. *Sci. and Cult.* 23: 659-660.

99. Needham, J. 1968. The development of botanical taxonomy in Chinese culture. *XIIth Congr. Intern. Hist. Sci.* Paris.

100. Neuhauser, M. B. 1952. Soybean sprouting. *Organic Gard.* 20: 12-13.

101. Nicol, C. M. 1940. Health conditions and health work in a famine area. *Ind. Med. Gaz.* 75: 662.

102. Nordfeldt, S. 1962. Influence of storage upon total tocopherols in wheat germs. Effect of germination upon total tocopherols in wheat. *K. Lantbrukshogskolans Ann.* 28: 181-188.

103. Ochse, J. J. 1931. *Vegetables of the Dutch East Indies*. Java.

104. Parijs, R. van. 1967. Quantitative changes of RNA, DNA, protein and dry matter in different organs of pea seedlings during germination and cell elongation. *Arch. Int. Physiol. Biochem.* 75: 125-138.

105. Patwardhan, V. N. 1952. Nutrition in India. *Ind. Jour. Med. Sci.* 6: 931. [*Review*]

106. Platt, C. S. 1944. Sprouted soybeans, mash and grains for emergency feeding of white leghorn pullets. *Poultry Sci.* 23: 505-508.

107. Porsild, A. E.; Harrington, C. R.; and Mulligan, G. A. 1967. *Lupinus arcticus* Wats. grown from seeds of Pleistocene age. *Science* 158: 113-114.

108. Quisumbing, E. 1951. *Medicinal Plants of the Philippines*. Manila.

109. Radhakrishnan, A. N.; Vaidyanathan, C. S.; and Giri, K. V. 1955. Nitrogenous constituents in plants: I. Free amino acids in leaves and leguminous seeds. *Jour. Ind. Inst. Sci.* 37: 178-194.

110. Ramakrishnan, C. V. 1957. Amino acid composition of crude and germinated guarseed flour protein (*Cyamopsis psoralioides*). *Experientia* 13: 78-79.

111. Read, B. E., trans. 1936. Li Shih-Chen, *Pen Ts'ao Kang Mu*, 1596. *Peking Nat. Hist. Bull.*, 1936.

112. Read, B. E. 1946. Famine foods listed in the *Chiu Huang Pen Ts'ao* giving their identity, nutritional values and notes on their preparation. *Henry Lister Inst. of Med. Res.*, Shanghai.

113. Rees, A. 1819. *The Cyclopaedia of Arts, Sciences and Literature*. London: W. Strahan.

114. Roddis, L. H. 1941. *A Short History of Nautical Medicine*. New York: Harper & Row.

115. Rohatgi, K.; Banerjee, M.; and Banerjee, S. 1955. Effect of germination on vitamin B_{12} values of pulses (leguminous seeds). *Jour. Nutrition* 56: 403-408.

116. Santos, F. O. 1922. Some plant sources of vitamins B and C. *Amer. Jour. Physiol.* 59: 310-334.

117. Schopfer, W. H. 1943. *Plants and Vitamins.* Waltham, Mass: Chronica Botanica Co.

118. Shaw, A. C., and Pascoe, L. C. 1949. Formation and distribution of vitamin C in the radicle and cotyledon of the broad bean (*Vicia faba*). *Nature* 164: 624.

119. Smith, A. H. 1918. Beer and scurvy, some notes from history. *Lancet* 2: 813-815.

120. Smith, F. P. 1871. Contributions towards the Materia Medica and Natural History of China, for the Use of Medical Missionaries and Native Medical Students. Shanghai.

121. Sreenivasan, A., and Wandrekar, S. D. 1950. Biosynthesis of vitamin C during germination. I. Effect of various environmental and cultural factors. *Proc. Ind. Acad. Sci. Sect. B*, 32: 143-163.

122. Sreenivasan, A., and Wandrekar, S. D. 1951. Excretion of vitamin C during germination of leguminous seeds. *Proc. Ind. Acad. Sci. Sect. B* 34: 267-271.

123. Stevenson, M. C. 1904. *The Zuñi Indians: their Mythology, Esoteric Societies, and Ceremonies.* Washington.

124. Stuart, G. A. 1911. *Chinese Materia Medica.* Shanghai: Amer. Presbyterian Mission Press.

125. Tobe, J. H. 1970. *Sprouts, Elixir of Life.* St. Catherine's, Ontario, Canada: Provoker Press.

126. Trelease, S. F., and Trelease, H. M. 1943. Sprouted soy and mungo beans. *N. Y. Bot. Gard. Jour.* 44: 254-260.

127. Tremazi, S. A. 1957. Ascorbic acid in some oleiferous brassicas cultivated in Pakistan. *Brit. Jour. Nutrition* 11: 1-4.

128. Van Dyne, F. O. 1950. Recipes for using soybeans ... fresh and dry. *Ill. Agric. Exper. Sta. Circ.* 662: 1-16.

129. Viktorov, D. P. 1914. The effect of low temperatures on the ascorbic acid content of wheat seedling. *Ref. Zh. Biol.*, 1964, No. 3G77.

130. Wai, K. N. T.; Bishop, J. C.; Mack, P. B.; and Cotton, R. H. 1947. The vitamin content of soybeans and soybean sprouts as a function of germination time. *Plant Physiol.* 22: 117-126.

131. Wats, R. C., and Eyles, C. M. E. 1932. Some sources of vitamin C in India. II. Germinated pulses, tomatoes, mangoes and bananas. *Ind. Jour. Med. Res.* 20: 89-106.

132. *The Wealth of India.* 1969. A Dictionary of Indian Raw Materials and Industrial Products. Vols. 2, 3, 8. New Delhi.

133. Went, F. W. 1963. *The Plants.* New York: Time-Life Books.

134. Went, F. W. 1955. The ecology of desert plants. *Scientific Amer.* 192: 68-75.

135. Whalley, B.; Derwyn, R.; and McKell, C. M. 1967. Interrelation of carbohydrate metabolism, seedling development and seedling growth rate of several species of *Phalaris. Agron. Jour.* 59: 223-226.

136. White, H. B., Jr. 1958. Fat utilization and composition in germinating cotton seeds. *Plant Physiol.* 33: 218-226.

137. Wiltshire, H. W. 1918. The value of germinated beans in the treatment of scurvy. *Lancet* 2: 811-813.

138. Winfield, G. F. 1948. *China: the Land and the People.* New York: Wm. Sloane.

139. Wu, C. H., and Fenton, F. 1953. Effect of sprouting and cooking of soybeans on palatability, lysine, tryptophane, thiamine, and ascorbic acid. *Food Res.* 18: 640-645.

140. Bircher-Benner, R. *Eating Your Way to Health.* London: Faber and Faber.

141. Hiatt, D. R., N. D. *The Sprouting of Seed for Fresh Food.* Coalmont, Tennessee: Message Press.

142. Hunter, B. T. 1961. *The Natural Foods Cookbook.* New York: Simon & Schuster, Inc.

143. Jensen, B., N. D. *Seeds and Sprouts for Life.* Escondido, California.

144. Jones, D. van G. 1968. *The Soybean Cookbook.* New York: Arc Books.

145. Mayer, A., and Poljakoff-Maber, A. 1963. *The Germination of Seeds.* Oxford: Pergamon Press.

146. Curtis, C. 1807. *An Account of the Disease of India as they appeared in the English Fleet.* Edinburgh.

INDEX

COOKBOOKS ON NATURAL HEALTH
. . . To Help You Eat Better for Less!

☐ AB** ..EW SPROUTS** (Martha H. Oliver)	**$1.50**
☐ **WHOLE GRAIN BAKING SAMPLER**	
(Beatrice Trum Hunter)	**$2.25**
☐ **MRS. APPLEYARD'S KITCHEN** (L.A. Kent)	**$3.50**
☐ **MRS. APPLEYARD'S SUMMER KITCHEN**	
(L.A. Kent & E.K. Gay)	**$3.50**
☐ **MRS. APPLEYARD'S WINTER KITCHEN**	
(L.A. Kent & E.K. Gay)	**$3.50**
☐ **BETTER FOODS FOR BETTER BABIES** (Gena Larson)	**$1.25**
☐ **GOOD FOODS THAT GO TOGETHER** (Elinor L. Smith)	**$2.95**
☐ **MEALS AND MENUS FOR ALL SEASONS** (Agnes Toms)	**$1.25**
☐ **NATURAL FOODS BLENDER COOKBOOK**	
(Frieda Nusz)	**$1.50**
☐ **GOLDEN HARVEST PRIZE WINNING RECIPES**	
(ed. by B.T. Hunter)	**$1.25**
☐ **SOYBEANS FOR HEALTH** (Philip Chen)	**$1.50**
☐ **FOOD AND FELLOWSHIP** (Elizabeth S. Pistole)	**95ᶜ**
☐ **MENNONITE COMMUNITY COOKBOOK**	
(Mary Emma Showalter)	**$1.25**
☐ **EAT THE WEEDS** (Ben Charles Harris)	**$1.50**

Buy them at your local health or book store or use this coupon.

Keats Publishing, Inc. (P.O. Box 876), New Canaan, Conn. 06840 75-C
Please send me the books I have checked above. I am enclosing
$___ (add 35ᶜ to cover postage and handling). Send check or
money order—no cash or C.O.D.'s please.

Mr/Mrs/Miss_____

Address _____

City _____ State _____ Zip_____
(Allow three weeks for delivery)